Mastering Physician Engagement

A Practical Guide to Achieving Shared Outcomes

Mastering Physician Engagement

A Practical Guide to Achieving Shared Outcomes

John W. Showalter, MD, MSIS

Leigh T. Williams, MHIIM, RHIA, CPC, CPHIMS

CRC Press
Taylor & Francis Group
Boca Raton London New York

CRC Press is an imprint of the
Taylor & Francis Group, an **informa** business

A PRODUCTIVITY PRESS BOOK

CRC Press
Taylor & Francis Group
6000 Broken Sound Parkway NW, Suite 300
Boca Raton, FL 33487-2742

First issued in paperback 2021

© 2017 by Taylor & Francis Group, LLC
CRC Press is an imprint of Taylor & Francis Group, an Informa business

ISBN-13: 978-1-4987-6882-5 (hbk)
ISBN-13: 978-1-03-217933-9 (pbk)
DOI: 10.1201/9781315367279

Publisher's Note

The publisher has gone to great lengths to ensure the quality of this reprint but points out that some imperfections in the original copies may be apparent.

Library of Congress Cataloging-in-Publication Data

Names: Showalter, John W., author. | Williams, Leigh T., author.
Title: Mastering physician engagement : a practical guide to achieving shared outcomes / John W. Showalter and Leigh T. Williams.
Description: Boca Raton : Taylor & Francis, 2017.
Identifiers: LCCN 2016032409 | ISBN 9781498768825 (hardback : alk. paper)
Subjects: LCSH: Hospital-physician relations. | Hospitals--Administration.
Classification: LCC RA971.9 .S56 2017 | DDC 362.11068--dc23
LC record available at https://lccn.loc.gov/2016032409

Visit the Taylor & Francis Web site at
http://www.taylorandfrancis.com

and the CRC Press Web site at
http://www.crcpress.com

Dedicated to the ones who inspire us to never
accept the limitations of today.

Abigail, Anna, JohnAndrew, Avangeline, and Adeline Showalter

Samuel and Thomas Williams

Contents

Foreword

When Leigh asked me to write a foreword for this book she said she wanted the book to be introduced by a "real doctor." At first I thought this was a humorous jab at John who is only a part-time hospitalist spending the majority of his time in informatics and analytics. In fact, John is an innovator, an outlier among physicians, one of the 2.5% you will read about in Chapter 7 on diffusion of innovation theory. I, on the other hand, am in the early majority or, on a good day, an early adopter. After reading the book, I realized Leigh was more likely referring to my learning style and my classic example as being different, not difficult. You see, I'm a neurosurgeon and as such, fall at the extremes of Kolb's convergent learning style. I have a tendency to act quickly, often too quickly, and have little respect for those who can't figure it out on their own.

As the reader will see in Chapter 6, I was a part of the formative process or perhaps an "unwitting victim" for the authors' model of physician engagement. They attempted to engage me in a documentation improvement program that faltered until the data they were presenting was transformed into actionable knowledge. Finally, able to understand the issues and metrics, I initiated effective documentation changes within my department. Over the course of a year, the Department of Neurosurgery was able to add an appreciable contribution to hospital margin without any significant change in the complexity or volume of our caseload. Furthermore, the improvement seen in the first year was carried over into the following year. This could never have been achieved without Leigh's ever enthusiastic, focused, results-oriented engagement and John's insightful, analytical and collaborative guidance.

I am convinced that this is a valid book, in part, because I have naively used many of the tactics described in my own efforts to engage fellow physicians and also because the theoretical basis is logical and the principles are sound. The authors organize and interrelate the concepts to form a cohesive model and support them with concrete, authentic examples. It is an easy read but the information is bountiful and complex. I plan to use it as a reference book to effectively engage my colleagues.

This book is not just for healthcare administrators. Physicians should read it as well to better understand themselves and to improve engagement of their colleagues. It would undoubtedly be a useful read for spouses, relatives and friends of physicians to enhance personal interactions in nonmedical situations.

Read, enjoy, and prepare to foster effective change in your organization.

Louis Harkey, MD, Robert R. Smith
Chair of Neurosurgery, University of Mississippi Medical Center

Introduction

Physician engagement has never been more important than it is today. Current fee-for-service models of care have had several unintended consequences, from unsustainable financial burdens to the proliferation of multi-drug-resistant bacteria, hospital-acquired conditions that kill thousands of people a year, and even physician shortages. Aging baby boomers further stress the system. We must become more efficient, do less harm, and keep people healthier. But, simply changing the system around physicians will not deliver the results we need to face these challenges. Physicians must be essential participants in changing the system to improve outcomes.

Physicians need our help. Providers are trained in how to care for patients, not the intricacies of healthcare reimbursement or mechanisms for care delivery. Physicians are key participants in healthcare, with a major impact on outcomes, and we must help guide them through the system as they help us care for our patients. They can't navigate modern healthcare reimbursement and delivery requirements without support, and we can't provide healthcare for our families and communities without them.

The complexity of the US healthcare system increases with each new law and regulation. Meaningful Use, the Affordable Care Act, Value-Based Purchasing, the Merit-Based Incentive Payment System, and the Medicare Access and CHIP Reauthorization Act of 2015 represent several thousands of pages describing how Medicare and Medicaid will make payments. They don't cover how private insurance carriers make payments or how to manage patient payments. Physicians can't take the time to learn about all of these rules, let alone rules from the Joint Commission, the Department of Health, or other accrediting agencies, without taking time away from patient care. In the face of physician shortages and outcomes that need improvement, it seems unwise to divert the focus of physicians away from patient care to interpreting rules. Since physicians are essential for effective change—and making them take time to interpret rules is unwise—everyone involved in healthcare supporting the physicians must assume the responsibility for aiding doctors in remaining compliant and being active participants in the shift to a pay-for-performance system. Unfortunately, we almost ubiquitously hear about how hard physicians are to engage. The purpose of this book is to help guide you through physician engagement to create substantive change.

Physicians are not challenging to collaborate with because they want to be, or even enjoy being, difficult. They are challenging because they have been taught to learn and make decisions differently from any other professionals. They spend years training to make independent decisions that directly impact patients' lives, frequently making life-and-death decisions. Understanding the psychology and learning style that physician training creates allows you to better understand your physician partners and develop communication strategies and other tactics to generate active physician engagement. Physician engagement will always be partially an art, but much like medicine, it is only partially art. There is science at the foundation. We have spent over 10 years studying that science and have integrated it into our approach.

Our approach—the heart of this book—is field tested and battle refined. When it comes to building physician consensus for organizational transformation, Dr. John Showalter has over a decade of hands-on experience. Lessons learned from Dr. Showalter's early missteps in his clinical informatics fellowship prepared him to lead a successful single-day implementation of an electronic health record (EHR) in four hospitals and over 90 clinic locations that affected over 1,500 providers. His experiences in establishing an award-winning Center for Informatics and Analytics as the chief health information officer are woven into the models we present. As a practicing internal medicine physician, Dr. Showalter has worked with hundreds of attending physicians and residents in teaching hospitals, observing daily the methods used to train and communicate with physicians. Dr. Showalter shares his insight as a physician, executive, researcher, and perpetual student of transformational change.

However, if we only covered how physicians can communicate with other physicians, we would be missing our primary audience. While Dr. Showalter is the perpetual student of the science, Leigh Williams is the master artist of transformational change through physician engagement.

As an expert administrator of the healthcare revenue cycle and information technology, Leigh's experience of executing the strategies in this book to engage physicians in professional and hospital billing and IT initiatives has generated millions of dollars of financial returns while improving patient outcomes. With a decade of experience working in both physician practices and hospitals, Leigh's approaches to involving physicians in the implementation of the International Classification of Diseases 10th Revision became the standard throughout the state of Mississippi. The clinical documentation excellence program that Leigh instituted directly impacted quality measures while improving physician use of an EHR. Leigh Williams has honed the science we present into practical and executable strategies and tactics that bring finesse to each engagement opportunity.

As a team, we have led physicians working in a complex academic medical center through some of the most challenging changes facing the US healthcare system and extended these practices to rural and community hospitals within our healthcare delivery system. This book will provide you with a toolkit to do the same.

The primary challenge of health system improvement is to keep everyone focused on the triple aim of better health, better healthcare, and lower costs despite multiple competing priorities and ever-changing regulations. Many of the priorities are important or urgent, thus driving the focus on the triple aim to the background. We challenge you to always keep the triple aim in mind, focusing on creating the best care systems for our communities. Throughout this book, you will learn new tactics and strategies you can apply in your daily work to help improve physician engagement and drive positive change. You will discover how physicians learn, how to motivate them, how to develop shared visions, and how to measure those visions. You will learn how to communicate data and define return on investment, as well as exploring frameworks to enhance your interactions with physicians. These tools are the paint, canvas, and artistic techniques we have used in painting our success. You will soon understand the science behind the art of physician engagement and be armed with the tools to paint your own success. Read, reread, and apply this book in your daily work. You have the ability to engage physicians in making healthcare better for all of us.

About the Authors

 **John Showalter, MD, MSIS** is a practicing internal medicine physician and chief health information officer at the University of Mississippi Medical Center. Also board certified in clinical informatics, John leads UMMC's Center for Analytics and Clinical Intelligence. He lives with his family in Jackson, Mississippi.

 **Leigh Williams, MHIIM, RHIA, CPHIMS, CHCIO-**Eligible is the senior health information technology leader responsible for business applications at the University of Virginia Health System and instructor of health informatics at the University of Mississippi. A veteran revenue cycle executive, she has served in leadership roles for both physician practice and hospital revenue cycle operations. Leigh lives with her family in Charlottesville, Virginia.

Chapter 1

Physicians Are Different, Not Difficult

Key Concepts

- There are four ways in which people learn new skills:
  - Diverging
  - Assimilating
  - Converging
  - Accommodating
- Physicians learn differently from most others because their medical training has taught them to be convergent learners.
- Convergent learners are hands-on, independent learners.
- Engaging physicians requires specific approaches that may be different from those useful for others involved in the same initiative.

1

It was a spring morning during the third year of my residency and I had just walked into the hospital when my pager vibrated. The message read, "Could you please come to the ICU to help with a central line?" Central lines are large IVs that are placed in a patient's neck or groin. I was comfortable with the procedure and was frequently asked to help by other residents, although in this case, "help" wasn't exactly the right word—the request was actually for me to do the procedure. The resident paging was either too busy, wasn't comfortable with the complexity of the patient, or had already failed at an attempt.

When I arrived at the ICU there was an intern (a first-year resident) who wanted to do the central line, but it would be the first one she had ever attempted. She had *assisted* with a central line or two, but never taken the lead. Given that residency training employs a "see one, do one, teach one" model of learning and I knew that she had already seen the procedure a few times, I approved her request. Maybe I should have found it odd that none of the other senior residents wanted to supervise her, but I didn't give it a second thought.

We both prepped for the procedure, covering ourselves in sterile gear from head to toe, and then I walked her through the procedure. We covered the patient with a sterile drape, sterilized the right side of his neck, used an ultrasound machine to find the vein, accessed the vein with a large needle, threaded a wire through the needle, slid the catheter over the wire, removed the wire, flushed the ports and stitched the line to the patient's neck. She did an excellent job on the first try with no complications.

As we walked out of the room, one of the other senior residents said, "I can't believe your let her do that line." I asked, "Why not?" and she responded, "The patient's platelets were 10 and we needed the access to give him a blood transfusion." I just shook my head. Platelets of 10 means that the patient was at an extreme risk of bleeding. If anything had gone wrong, it would have been very hard to stop the bleeding, and a second attempt at the procedure would have been very difficult, while a delay in the procedure might have been fatal. I silently breathed a sigh of relief that everything had gone well.

Does it seem strange to you that no one raised a red flag? That no one suggested we stop or wait for an experienced fellow or attending physician? There was certainly time to raise the alarm—it takes 15 minutes to prep for the procedure. Yet, not one of the other senior residents pulled me aside and suggested I wait or do the procedure myself, even knowing how risky the procedure was.

Why Not?

Because physicians learn by *doing*, and we learn by doing it *ourselves*. No one can hold the needle for you. No one else can feel the slight pop when the needle enters the vein. Since she might have to place a central line in the future in a patient at high risk for bleeding, no one flinched at her first attempt being a high-risk procedure. There is a slow shift toward starting with simulation laboratories to decrease complications, but medical students and residents are still taught through *experience*. This training approach— and even the very way students are selected for admission to medical school—results in a group that is unique.

That uniqueness is the focus of this chapter.

Exploring the unique characteristics and qualities of physicians requires us to look at how adults acquire new skills. The best psychological framework for this discussion is Kolb's Experiential Learning Theory and its Learning Styles framework.[1] It is important to note that these are not the learning styles you are most likely familiar with from school, such as visual, aural, or verbal. Kolb's framework focuses on the balance between how much a person learns independently through activities such as reading and how much is learned by doing. "Learning style describes the unique ways that individuals spiral through the learning cycle based on their preference for the four different learning modes: Concrete Experience (CE), Reflective Observation (RO), Abstract Conceptualization (AC), and Active Experimentation (AE). Because of our genetic makeup, our particular life experiences, and the demands of our present environment, we develop a preferred way of choosing among these four learning modes."[1] In the framework depicted graphically in Figure 1.1, all learning exists on these two spectrums, and groups or individuals can be placed along the spectrum. Where a person lands on this spectrum is influenced by several factors,

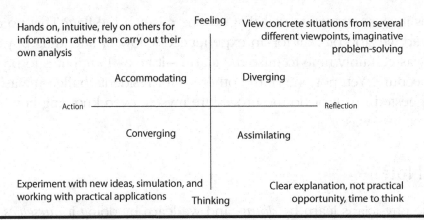

Figure 1.1 **Kolb's Learning Styles illustrate the four quadrants that are created when the spectrums are combined. Starting at the upper right and going clockwise, the four distinct learning styles are Diverging, Assimilating, Converging, and Accommodating. (From Kolb, A. and D. Kolb,** *The Kolb Learning Style Inventory: Version 3.1, 2005 Technical Specifications.* **Hay Resources Direct, Boston, MA, 2005.)**

including educational experiences, basic cognitive skills make-up, and social environments. These three factors align to place physicians in a group by themselves.

The first of the two spectrums runs from an individual learning purely alone to an individual learning only from others. This spectrum creates classic stereotypes: at one extreme we have the introverted bookworm, and at the other is the outgoing athlete. As with most stereotypes, this is a gross oversimplification. The introvert may learn a great deal from professors or individuals in a small study group, and the athlete may spend countless hours watching films or running drills independently.

What matters here is not the environment where the skill is executed, but rather, how much an individual relies on others to understand and acquire a new skill. In Kolb's framework, this spectrum is the vertical axis. The lower portion of the axis is "thinking," meaning that the person learns through problem-solving and understanding analytical models. Think of a research scientist, a computer programmer, or a musician. The upper portion is "feeling," representing that the person learns through intuition and gut instinct, like artists, writers, and designers. Intrinsically, thinking is an *independent* activity that relies on what's going on inside the learner's mind, while intuition and gut instinct are frequently influenced by others, absorbing cues and information from other people.

The second spectrum, displayed as the horizontal axis, runs from those who only learn by "doing" to those who only learn by reflecting on what others have done. The left side of the axis is action and the right is reflection. In my family, I am the doer and rarely start with the instructions; I dive right in with my hands and figure it out myself as I work with the pieces or process. A good friend comes from the other end of the spectrum and approaches a new task with a full review of the instructions and an inventory of the pieces before beginning. Almost no one exists at the extremes of these spectrums, but they serve as a measure against which we can plot how an individual most often learns. We are also able to track how learning style changes based on environmental and social influences.

Diverging learners acquire new skills through intuition, imagination, listening, and personalized feedback. Classically, they are considered creative and have a broad range of interests, causing them to excel in brainstorming. They have an open approach to problem-solving and approach concrete problems from multiple points of view. There is actually a simple test to identify divergent thinkers. In two minutes, list all the uses for a brick. Divergent thinkers will give a great number of answers that include atypical uses, such as breaking a window or painting the brick for decoration. Because they identify multiple solutions/outcomes to problems, it can be difficult for divergent learners to make decisions; in fact, it is safe to say that this group is indecisive, and they may even appear haphazard, because decisions are very fluid as new thoughts and concepts occur to them.

Assimilating learners think long and deeply about existing knowledge, applying it to theories and analytical models. They apply information from books and lectures to abstract concepts to make logical sense of the information. The focus is on sound reasoning rather than practical application. While others may perceive assimilating learners as slow to take action, in reality, most assimilating learners have little problem taking action once a decision has been made; however, they frequently take their time to analyze a problem from multiple frameworks before coming to a decision. Assimilating learners will also examine new evidence and change their decisions in light of compelling feedback.

Those with a converging learning style learn predominately by independent action, that is, hands-on experimentation, simulations, and other practical applications of knowledge. They gravitate toward technical tasks rather than social or interpersonal problems and are practical problem solvers with well-developed decision-making skills. Once converging learners make a decision, they are resolute in their conviction, because the decision was reached only after they had personally tested their hypothesis. Converging learners are slow to respond to new evidence, because they must personally test all new feedback to determine whether it is of value and whether it should be integrated into their decision-making.

Accommodating learners gather information from other people rather than doing their own analysis. They act on intuition instead of logical analysis and acquire new skills mostly through hands-on experience and tackling new challenges. They are action oriented and prefer to work in groups. Accommodating learners are influenced by others in their decision-making, often relying on peers and opinion leaders to inform their choices and actions. Peer influences and feedback will also cause accommodating learners to change their minds.

Relatively little research has been done to determine the learning style distribution in the general population. However, a significant amount of research has been completed on the dominant learning styles within professions. It is this work that begins to show just how unique physicians are with regard to acquiring new skills. At this point, it is essential to note that these learning styles are exclusionary in the framework; that is, a person is assigned to only one group. In reality, most people learn in all four ways, and the framework is describing an individual's preferred learning style, or the way in which individuals most easily learn. The exclusionary nature of the framework is one of its greatest limitations; however, this concern has little impact on the topic of physicians.

When we examine the dominant learning style in a profession (Figure 1.2), it makes sense in terms of how we generally characterize those groups. Creative professions, such as fine arts and writing, are divergent.

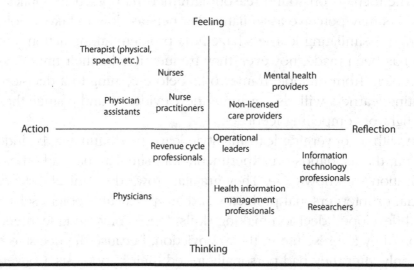

Figure 1.2 Kolb's learning styles as applied to healthcare professionals.

Logic-oriented professions such as scientific research and information technology are assimilating. People-oriented professions such as teaching and nursing are accommodating. Only two groups exist in the converging quadrant—revenue cycle professionals including financial accountants and physicians—and physicians are much more solidly in that quadrant. Physicians are the only group that learns new skills almost exclusively by doing things by themselves.

Physicians are difficult to engage because they are different; it is this difference that leads others to perceive them as difficult. Physicians are not difficult on purpose or out of spite. They are difficult because they are selected and trained to be different. Understanding this difference is the first step toward real engagement.

When we explore the history of medical education and training, we begin to understand the difference that starts with physician selection. Many are hopeful that we are currently in a renaissance of medical education, with a growing focus on humanity and its role in patient-centric care. However, we are only in the early stages of this renaissance, with its beginnings traced back to the mid-2000s; in truth, medical education has undergone little change in the last 100 years.

At the turn of the twentieth century, medical education in the United States was a free-for-all of unregulated private institutions, thought to be creating an excess supply of doctors who were poorly trained. That changed in 1910 with the publication of the Flexner Report. Flexner's scathing review of US medical education evaluated the system largely against the German model of medical education, which appraised schools based on admission requirements, laboratory facilities, and focus on medicine as a science. The report resulted in the closure of over 30% of US medical schools; for the next 100 years, medical education focused on medicine as a science and the advancement of knowledge.

This established the paradigm still in place today, with medical school entrance requiring an undergraduate degree, successful completion of laboratory and science education before the start of clinical training, and a focus on research and publication. A 100 year review of the Flexner Report published in the *Yale Journal of Biology and Medicine* concluded: "the profession's infatuation with the hyper-rational world of German medicine created an excellence in science that was not balanced by a comparable excellence in clinical caring."

This hyper-rationality is evident in the selection of medical students. As displayed in Figure 1.3, a 1995 study of students in the medical profession

	Diverging	Assimilating	Converging	Accommodating
Medical students	8%	26%	45%	21%
Nursing students	27.9%	18.8%	27.4%	25.8%

Figure 1.3   Distribution of medical and nursing students across learning styles. (From Lynch, T. et al., *American Journal of Surgery,* **176, 62–66, 1998, for medical students; Cavanagh, S.H. et al.,** *Nurse Education Today,* **15, 177–183, 1995 for nursing students.)**

showed that over 70% of medical students were assimilating or converging learners, with a remarkable 45% of them converging. It is even more noteworthy in comparison with the other medical professional students in the study: nurses. Nursing students were almost evenly distributed across the four learning styles.

The selection of students who will succeed and integrate into a hyperrational world begins the physician's journey to join a group of professionals who learn like no others. This journey continues after medical school as the new physicians enter and complete their clinical training as residents. Clinical training after medical school consists of residencies and fellowships. This training is essentially a multi-year apprenticeship. This period of supervised practice takes a minimum of 3 years, but can be as long as 9, depending on the physician's specialty. During the first year of training, they are referred to as *interns*; during additional training, they are *senior residents*; and finally, physicians doing additional training in specialty programs are known as *fellows*.

Supervised practice is a vastly different educational model for professionals who have spent most of their lives succeeding in a classroom environment. These new educational experiences and social interactions with their supervising physicians (attending physicians) continue to shape their learning styles. A 2007 study of surgical residents demonstrated that the experiences of supervised practice did affect the learning style of the residents (Figure 1.4). The learning styles among interns were very similar to those of medical students, with 70% assimilating and converging, and 49% converging. However, after 5 years of training, 81% were assimilating and converging, with 67% converging; two-thirds of physicians in the study were converging learners. Two-thirds of the physicians studied acquired new skills

Surgical residency year	Diverging	Assimilating	Converging	Accommodating
1	14%	21%	49%	17%
2	14%	21%	46%	18%
3	2%	15%	66%	17%
4	13%	15%	61%	11%
5	10%	14%	67%	10%

Figure 1.4 Changes in learning style for physician learners during the 5 years of residency. (From Mammen, J.M.V. et al., *Journal of Surgical Education*, 64, 386–389, 2007.)

by doing procedures, completing simulations, and active experimentation; no other profession comes close to this proportion.

Residency encourages this transition of learning style, because the goal of the 100-year-old model is to create practitioners who can treat patients independently with little peer support. A century ago, a provider had only a shelf of books and himself to guide the treatment of patients; there was very little peer support. Self-reliance was, and is, recognized as a hallmark of a great physician.

Physicians are remarkably homogeneous in their learning styles. Over 75% learn independently, and over 75% learn best with hands-on activities. Classic engagement strategies do not play to these strengths. Think back to the last time you tried to engage a physician to make a change; remember, change requires performing a new skill. Did you focus on hands-on experiences that were directly relevant to the provider's work? Did you give the provider a chance to perform the new behavior themselves? Did you use simulation or trial the new workflow?

If you answered yes, I bet you were successful. If you answered no, you are not alone, and I bet you were disappointed in your results. At that time, you probably thought it was just typical *difficult* physician behavior, but now you see that it was probably the very typical *different* physician learning style.

References

1. Kolb, A. and D. Kolb. 2012. Kolb's learning styles. In *Encyclopedia of the Sciences of Learning*, ed. N. M. Seel, 1698–1703. Berlin: Springer U.S.
2. Lynch, T., N. Woelfl, D. Steele, and C. Hanssen. 1998. Learning style influences student learning performance. *American Journal of Surgery*. Vol. 176, 62–66.
3. Cavanagh, S. H., K. Hogan, and T. Ramgopal. 1995. The assessment of student nurse learning styles using the Kolb learning styles inventory. *Nurse Education Today*. Vol. 15, 177–183.
4. Mammen, J. M. V., D. R. Fischer, A. Anderson, L. E. James, M. S. Nussbaum, R. H. Bower, and T. A. Pritts. 2007. Learning styles vary among general surgery residents: Analysis of 12 years of data. *Journal of Surgical Education*. Vol. 64, 6, 386–389.

Chapter 2

Promoting Adoption among Physicians

Key Concepts

- Due to their medical training, physicians are taught not to be heavily influenced by peer pressure.
- To readily comply with a change, physicians need to personally experience the benefit of the change through personally witnessing or experiencing the benefit.
- Physicians don't experience a dramatic tipping point in the adoption curve, because they don't initiate change just because someone else did.
- Physicians have three main drivers:
  - The desire to try something new
  - The desire to remain influential
  - A fear of failure
- Physicians will not adopt a change till they are confident that they will personally succeed.

In April 1867, Joseph Lister published his pioneering work on infection control. The inspiration for oral care disinfectant Listerine, Lister's studies actually revolved around the care of open fractures. At that time, if you were unlucky enough to fracture a limb in such a way that the bone was sticking out, the odds were not in your favor. Due to high rates of infection in the limb that spread throughout the body and were often fatal, physicians usually treated this type of fracture with amputation. This wasn't a guarantee that you would survive; in fact, 45% of surgical patients in the latter half of the nineteenth century would die from infection.

Lister approached his work with the expectation that there was a better way to address the problem; what if they could save the limb by preventing the infection in the first place? In his seminal study, Lister applied carbonic acid to open fractures prior to surgery to test its efficacy in reducing or eliminating infections in the patient. In many cases, amputation was avoided altogether. When amputation was necessary, mortality decreased dramatically from 45% to 15%. In the first published study that proved that infections—and even death—from wounds and surgical sites could be avoided, Lister saved lives and propelled the treatment of injuries into the modern era.

It has been nearly 150 years since Lister's publication indicating that a focus on infection control saves lives and reduces complications, yet the adoption of basic antiseptic measures, such as handwashing, still hasn't reached the tipping point in today's hospitals. Physicians have continually demonstrated poor compliance with basic handwashing protocols, while infection control remains a top priority for hospitals. As observed in published studies as recently as 2015,[1] the compliance rates for physicians can be as low as 53% of the time when handwashing is required as a basic infection-control measure.[2] Knowledge and social pressures do not yet outweigh the barriers to handwashing for physicians, so despite having a deep and long-standing understanding of the issue, as well as motivation to provide the best care for their patients, many physicians remain largely non-compliant. Handwashing is the most basic component of antisepsis, and after a century and a half, many physicians perform this skill adequately only half of the time.

To say that physicians can be slow to adopt may be a gross understatement. However, to understand their slow adoption, we need to look at how physicians adopt new technologies. Let's consider one of the greatest technology adoptions in the history of medicine: inhaled anesthesia.

In September 1846, the first recorded surgery using an inhaled anesthetic took place when the dentist William Morton used an ether-soaked handkerchief to sedate a patient and painlessly remove a tooth. After a few more successes and a public demonstration, Morton's discovery was quickly communicated around the world. Within 20 years, inhaled anesthetic in the form of ether or chloroform was widely used. Contrary to the popular belief that most Civil War field hospitals performed amputations without anesthesia, it is estimated that inhaled anesthesia was used up to 75% of the time. By the mid-1870s, inhaled anesthesia was the surgical standard of care, enjoying broad adoption and physician compliance.

What was it about inhaled anesthesia that resulted in its being adopted so quickly compared with handwashing?

The answer is simple: anesthesia demonstrated immediate benefits for both the physician and the patient. The patient was sedated, did not feel pain, and thus did not move. The surgeon could take more time doing the procedure. It was easy to experiment and see success. If a physician wasn't willing to try it on a patient, it could be tried on a cat or a pig. Ether and handkerchiefs were simple to obtain. Once a subject, human or otherwise, woke up after being exposed to ether or chloroform, physicians were eager to try it in surgery. The pain from surgery disturbed both the patient and the physician, so avoiding it was an easy choice.

Handwashing has none of those components. Washing your hands does not prevent something easy to witness, such as pain; it prevents microscopic organisms from being transferred to a patient, which may result in an infection at a later date. Handwashing does not help the physician perform her tasks; rather, it actually adds time every time she sees a patient. Given the rarity with which a single event can be tied to a specific infection, it is very difficult to experiment with handwashing to prove its effectiveness. There is more than sufficient research to demonstrate that improved handwashing compliance reduces infections in hospitals, but it is next to impossible to prove that infections are caused by any one event. Given these limitations and what we know about how physicians learn, is it any wonder that physicians haven't adopted the skill of universal handwashing?

The spread of a new idea or technology is a highly social activity, and it is one of the most studied areas of social science. Over 4,000 research articles have been published on the topic in the last 70 years. The results of these studies are so consistent that a cohesive theory has been developed to explain them: the Diffusion of Innovation Theory. The theory of the diffusion of innovation addresses how a new idea or invention comes to be used by a significant portion of the population. It explores the psychology, social interactions, personality traits, and characteristics of the innovation that propel mass adoption. Two of the most significant aspects of the theory are its definition of innovation and the description of the adoption tipping point.

According to the theory, an innovation is an idea, practice, or object that is *perceived as new* by an individual or other unit of adoption. It matters little, as far as human behavior is concerned, whether or not an idea is "objectively" new as measured by the lapse of time since its first use or discovery. Put more simply: if it is new to you, it is an innovation from your perspective. From a physician engagement perspective, this means that every time you want them to do something different, it is an innovation to them.

The tipping point is the level of adoption at which the social pressure to adopt outweighs the perceived barriers to adoption; once the tipping point is reached, the rate of adoption rapidly increases. Most adoption efforts target the tipping point as their goal, based on the belief that the innovation will become the norm once the tipping point is reached.

Across the vast array of innovations that have been studied, there is amazing consistency in how they diffuse through a population. This consistency has led to the realization that when percentage adoption is plotted against time, an S-shaped curve is created (Figure 2.1). The curve demonstrates the initially slow rate of adoption, followed by an increasing rate as the innovation becomes more commonplace, the rapid rate of adoption near the tipping point, and finally, the slow rate of adoption by the final individual. The tipping point—and this S-curve—are critical for understanding the difficulties with engaging physicians.

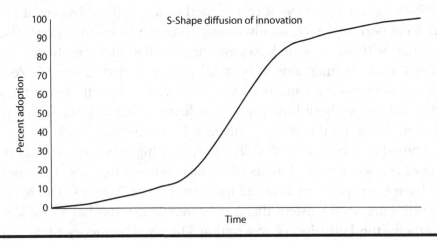

Figure 2.1   The diffusion of innovation curve.

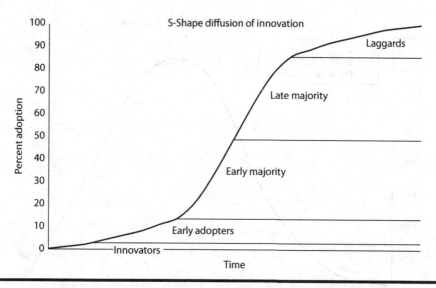

Figure 2.2   The diffusion of innovation curve depicting adoption groups.

In addition to the predictable average adoption S-curve, groups involved in adoption at various points in the curve have been characterized (Figure 2.2). There are five groups involved in the diffusion of innovation: innovators, early adopters, early majority, late majority, and laggards.

■ Innovators have a wide social network, are interested in new things, have a high tolerance for failure and new ideas, and are more interested in trying things than in being right.

■ Early adopters have frequent interactions with the innovators, but are selective about what they try/endorse. They are motivated by maintaining/developing their influence as opinion leaders, so they are interested in being right about the value of an innovation before they adopt.

■ The early majority wait for opinion leaders (early adopters) to adopt and be successful. They are motivated by social pressure. Once opinion leaders demonstrate success, the early majority quickly begin adopting so they aren't late to the party.

■ The late majority are heavily influenced by social pressures but are skeptical, have a low tolerance of uncertainty, and need to understand the personal benefits of adopting. They rapidly adopt once the early majority have demonstrated consistent success.

■ Laggards have a fear of failure and require assurances of success. They will only adopt new innovations when that adoption is necessary for their own success.

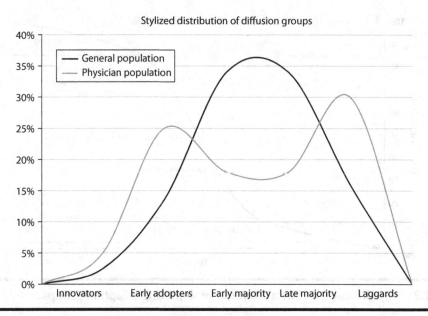

Figure 2.3   The adoption group distribution depicting how physicians differ from the general population.

Innovators are the smallest portion of the population, representing only about 2.5% of the population. They are internally motivated, and are most likely to be converging or accommodating learners. Early adopters make up approximately 13.5% of the population and laggards 16%. This combined 32% of the population are internally motivated and minimally influenced by social pressure; as a group, early adopters and laggards are most likely to be converging or assimilating learners. The early majority and late majority are heavily influenced to adopt based on social pressures, and combined, they represent the remaining 68% of the total population. They are the divergent and accommodating learners.

When we again look at nursing students, this distribution of social influence holds true; almost 64% of nursing students were divergent or accommodating learners. However, when we look at physician trainees who are about to enter independent medical practice, only 20% are divergent or accommodating learners. That means that only about 20% of physicians have adoption characteristics similar to the early and late majority, and the other 80% are more like innovators, early adopters, or laggards (Figure 2.3).

The shift from 68% of the population being motivated by social influence to just 20% who are influenced by social pressure blunts—and even eliminates—the effect of the tipping point. The result is that the physician adoption curve is much less S-shaped and much more linear (Figure 2.4).

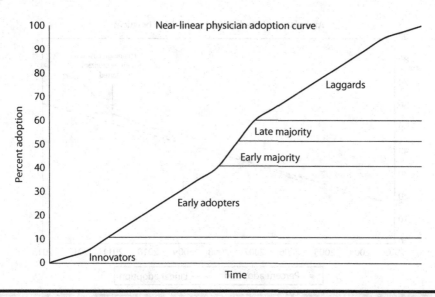

Figure 2.4   The physicians' diffusion of innovation curve depicting their adoption groups.

The largest physician technology adoption effort of this century, the adoption of electronic health records (EHRs), provides a great example of this phenomenon. The adoption of EHRs by health systems does not necessarily reflect the adoption patterns of individual physicians, so we will look at the adoption of EHRs by office-based practices. The rate of EHR adoption was stagnant at the turn of the century, but has been almost constant at a little more than 6% since 2005 (Figure 2.5). Between 2005 and 2013, 54.5% of office-based physicians adopted an EHR, bringing the total from 23.9% to 78.4%. For 6 of those 8 years, adoption increased between 5.3% and 7.2%. 2010 was a slow year, at 2.7%. Due to the incentives from Meaningful Use, 2012 was a year of high adoption, at 14.1%. However, 2013 was at only 6.6%. It is possible to argue that 2012 was a tipping point, but an increase of 6.9% for 1 year, especially with millions of dollars of incentive payments, is a greatly blunted tipping point.

The linear nature of the adoption curve means that adoption by physicians takes much longer than classic diffusion theory would predict.

The distribution of physician learning styles not only blunts the tipping point, it also means that the majority of physicians have one of three main drivers: the desire to try something new (innovators); the desire to remain influential with their peers (early adopters); or a fear of failure (laggards).

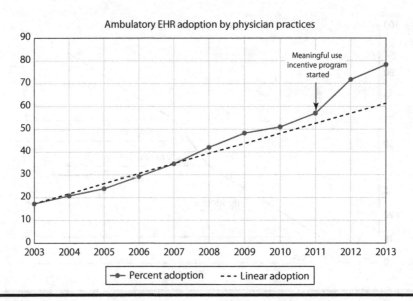

Figure 2.5   U.S. office-based physicians with EHRs by year. The chart shows a comparison of physician office adoption of "any" EHR systems versus a linear adoption model between 2001 and 2013, according to the National Center for Health Statistics. (From CDC/NCHS. National Ambulatory Medical Care Survey, Electronic Health Records Survey. NCHS Data Brief no. 143 (January 2014). www.cdc.gov/nchs/data/databriefs/db143.pdf [Accessed July 1, 2016.])

Given that early adopters and laggards will greatly outnumber innovators, the motivators for these groups will be the primary drivers of adoption for most physicians. The primary factor that all of these groups have in common is being confident of success.

How much time do you spend trying to convince physicians that they *should* versus convincing them that they *can*, and can do so in a way that will make them highly successful?

Anesthesia was the perfect innovation to diffuse through a group whose adoption is dominated by confidence in success. One of the greatest accounts of anesthesia during the nineteenth century was the amputation of General Stonewall Jackson's arm after injury by a round ball. The injury ultimately led to his death. With great stoicism, the general agreed to the amputation and the administration of chloroform. Per the accountings of the surgeon, "Chloroform was then administered, and as he began to feel its effects, and its relief to the pain he was suffering, he exclaimed: 'What an infinite blessing,' and continued to repeat the word 'blessing,' until he became insensible."[4]

Which physician didn't want to write to his colleague about how amazing it was to have a patient lie still and feel no pain during a procedure? Which physician didn't want to be the first to demonstrate it in the surgical theater? Most patients died from surgery and felt a great deal of pain during the procedure. Success was simply relief of pain and that the patient lay still—and anesthesia did both.

The rapid diffusion of anesthesia has been attributed to the benefits it provided to the patient and physician, and that certainly played a part. But it is likely that physicians' confidence in their own ability to administer anesthesia—and the effectiveness of this new technology to provide the outcome they desired—had even more to do with its rapid adoption.

So, what's so complicated about handwashing? It's a simple skill— physicians can certainly perform it successfully. Why haven't they adopted this straightforward, uncomplicated innovation to care for their patients? Perhaps execution of a task is not what drives physicians.

References

1. Redelmeier, D. and E. Shafir. 2015. Why even good physicians do not wash their hands. *BMJ Quality and Safety Online First.* doi:10.1136/bmjqs-2015-004319 (Accessed July 1, 2016).
2. Jitesh Kar, J., K. Brown, T. Walker, J. Sheiner, J. Headley, A. Murphy, S. Cooper, Enedra A.-McBride, M. Morales, and P. Schulz. 2014. Quality improvement project on handwashing at Memorial Hermann Hospital. *Neurology.* Vol. 82 (10 Suppl), P4.291.
3. CDC/NCHS. National Ambulatory Medical Care Survey, Electronic Health Records Survey. NCHS Data Brief no. 143 (January 2014). www.cdc.gov/nchs/data/databriefs/db143.pdf (Accessed July 1, 2016).
4. McGuire, H. Stonewall Jackson 1824–1863. Southern Historical Society Papers. http://americancivilwar.com/south/stonewall_jackson_death.html (Accessed July 1, 2016).
5. Sherman, M. Ed. 1998. *Medical Device Packaging Handbook,* 2nd edition. Boco Raton, FL: CRC Press.

Chapter 3

Theory of Planned Behavior

Key Concepts

- Physicians respond to intrinsic, not extrinsic, motivation.
  - Intrinsic motivation is felt internally, coming from an internal sense of purpose.
  - Extrinsic motivation is based on penalties or rewards as the result of an external outcome.
- Understanding the intrinsic motivations of the physicians you are working with is essential to developing successful engagement programs.
- The theory of planned behavior provides a road map for influencing intrinsic motivations.
- Positive deviance provides a technique for identifying individuals who are being successful so that you can determine factors that may be useful in influencing the intrinsic motivations of others.

It's a common misconception that physicians drive sporty cars. Some do, but most are a bit more practical, especially those of us with five children. That's why I was driving a minivan when I got pulled over for speeding. I was cruising through Virginia on a major highway, 11 mph over the speed limit, so I wasn't shocked when I got pulled over by a county trooper. It wasn't that I didn't know the speed limit, or that I didn't know how fast I was going. It wasn't that I was incapable of controlling my speed. It was mainly that I didn't care; I was driving at a speed where I felt safe and comfortable just over 10 mph above the posted limit. And I was fully prepared to pay a fine if I was stopped.

What I wasn't prepared for was a citation for reckless driving.

In Virginia, driving at speeds more than 10 mph above the posted highway limits is considered reckless driving. After I paid the legal fees and the lawyer, attended driving school, and paid the citation fine, the citation was reissued as a simple speeding ticket. At just under $2,000, that was the most expensive speeding ticket I have ever received. The Commonwealth of Virginia was effective at changing my behavior—in Virginia. I will never speed in Virginia again. Mostly because I will never drive in Virginia again, unless I absolutely have to do so.

Extrinsic motivators can be every effective in eliciting specific behavioral changes, but they rarely foster engagement. The proverbial carrot and stick only gets the horse to where the carrot is or the stick isn't. American Pharaoh didn't become the Triple Crown winner because he wanted a carrot at the finish line. His trainers developed a horse who wanted to win.

All too frequently, attempts at physician engagement are built around financial incentives and penalties. These are just more carrots and sticks. This method creates physicians who do just well enough to be rewarded (or avoid being penalized). It entirely fails to create physicians who want to win.

Meaningful Use, Hospital-Acquired Conditions and the Hospital Readmissions Reduction Program are all financial incentive and penalty programs from the Centers for Medicare and Medicaid Services (CMS). Each program has effectively produced the prescribed outcome. Meaningful Use paid physicians to implement and use electronic health records (EHRs) in a way that met predetermined criteria and has successfully driven the adoption of

EHRs. The Office of the National Coordinator reports that adoption rates for EHRs have increased to over 93% of hospitals and more than 78% of office-based physicians.[1] The Healthcare-Acquired Conditions program, whereby CMS reduced payments when patients developed certain conditions during their hospital stay, deserves at least partial credit for the 46% reduction in central line–associated bloodstream infections and the 19% reduction in surgical site infections between 2008 and 2013.[2] The readmissions reduction program reduced all payments to a hospital that was found to have excess readmissions for certain conditions and significantly contributed to a 6%–10% reduction in readmission for those conditions.[2]

These gains are obviously good for patients. Reduced harm events during a hospitalization and fewer patients needing to return to a hospital after discharge are laudable gains. However, these programs have not been a physician call to arms against hospital-acquired infections or improved home care for the chronically ill. Instead, health systems have been running from the stick and stopping once they are out of reach. The U.S. healthcare system needs to eliminate the remaining 54% of central line–associated bloodstream infections and 81% more surgical site infections. We won't do that based on health systems and physicians trying to stay one step ahead of the switch.

Health systems that have committed to reducing readmissions have demonstrated a 44% reduction in readmissions compared with the 6%–10% reduction due to the CMS program. Comprehensive clinical programs have reduced surgical site infections by 33% and central line infections by 81%, significantly more than the 19% and 46% reductions due to the CMS program.[2]

So how do we create physicians who want to win? We start with understanding what truly drives them.

Between 1994 and 2012, there was a 53% reduction in risk-adjusted mortality for coronary artery bypass graft (CABG) surgery in Pennsylvania.[3] An initial 30% reduction occurred between 1994 and 2000. There were several factors driving this change: financial incentives; technology improvements; and the publication of a "CABG quality score card" by the Pennsylvania HealthCare Cost Containment Council (PHC4), which allowed both patients and physicians to see how well individual surgeons performed with regard to outcomes from CABG surgery.

John Kolstad, PhD, assistant professor of healthcare management at the Wharton School of Business, tackled the problem of teasing out the impact of physician motivation in the improvement of CABG outcomes. In a retrospective analysis of the initial 30% improvement, he used economic theories to model the impact of Pennsylvania publishing the quality score card.[4] He first determined how much mortality should have improved due just to advances in practice. Based on the model, without the publication of the scorecard, risk-adjusted mortality would have fallen by only 3.3%. Next, he calculated the impact of extrinsic motivations, such as financial motivations. Extrinsic motivations led to an additional 5.6% reduction. The remaining 21% of improvement was due to intrinsic motivation.

Over two-thirds of the reduction in mortality was due to surgeons simply wanting to do better. Intrinsic motivation was almost four times as powerful as extrinsic motivation. As he dug deeper into the data, the impact of publishing the data got even more interesting. He analyzed the improvement of individual physicians who found out that they had worse than average, average, or better than average outcomes. All three groups reduced mortality over the period studied. However, the top performers improved twice as much as average surgeons. Finding that they were the best spurred them on to be even better. Perhaps less shocking, but even more significant, was that the bottom performers improved almost 2.5 times more than the best performers and showed five times more improvement than the average performers. Based on Kolstad's analysis, one of the most impactful events was a physician finding out that they had the worst outcomes at the hospital where they practiced.

Kolstad's analysis is an excellent demonstration of how you produce physicians who want to win: connect with what they care about most— delivering good patient care. Physicians don't wake up and say, "I want to be the worst surgeon," or "I don't care if someone treats patients better than I do." Physicians are motivated by great patient care and great patient outcomes. Having led several physician change initiatives, my mantra is "If I can convince physicians that hitting them with a sledge hammer is good for their patients, physicians will let me hit them with a sledge hammer." It is a bit extreme, but it keeps my focus on the most significant and important challenge: convincing physicians that change is good for their patients. As Kolstad's analysis demonstrates, convincing physicians that change is good for their patients is four times more powerful than convincing them that it is good for them. But there is the rub; it needs to actually be good for their patients. They also need to know how to accomplish the improvement.

In light of Kolstad's analysis, it is interesting to note that the CMS improvement programs for readmissions,[5] central line–associated bloodstream infections, and surgical site infections[5] achieved approximately 23%, 57%, and 58%, respectively, of the potential improvements. This indicates that physicians feel little intrinsic motivation to improve readmissions, and that the programs are only partially engaging physicians' intrinsic motivations with regard to hospital-acquired conditions. In our experience, the lack of intrinsic motivation with these programs is largely due to the delayed reporting of outcomes. The data is at least two years old. Old data is hard to trust and thus easy to ignore, and having to wait two years to see any impact allows other priorities to take precedence.

Understanding how Kolstad's analysis intersects with a lack of handwashing is an excellent window into physician engagement and intrinsic motivation. As described in Chapter 2, handwashing remains dismally low despite almost 200 years of evidence to support the practice. Certainly, physicians must know that it is good for their patients. Indeed, they do. When Pittet et al. published "Hand hygiene among physicians: Performance, beliefs, and perceptions" in the *Annals of Internal Medicine* in 2014, 92% of physicians perceived hand hygiene as a useful measure to prevent healthcare-associated infections.[6] However, compliance with handwashing was only 57%. Pittet et al.'s paper was designed to tease apart this disconnect by surveying the physicians at their hospital. The intention to perform a behavior is directly related to actually performing the behavior, and only 77% of physicians intended to perform hand hygiene as recommended.

How can only three out of four physicians intend to wash their hands? First, only 49% of physicians believe that other physicians wash their hands. Second, only 31% of physicians think it is important to be a role model with regard to washing hands. Third, 67% perceive handwashing during patient care as a difficult task. And finally, only 35% believe that they know the recommended guidelines for handwashing.[6] In summary, this means that physicians don't know when they should wash their hands, find it difficult to do so while taking care of patients, and believe that other physicians don't wash their hands and don't care if they do. Given those figures, it is surprising that almost 80% of physicians intend to wash their hands, but it is not surprising that it only happens 57% of the time.

An understanding of the theory of planned behavior is needed to further explore Pittet et al.'s findings, as well as to explain why extrinsic factors are ineffective at engaging physicians. The theory of planned behavior, like most psychological theories, is fairly complex, but it can be summarized like this: when a person has the option of whether or not to take an action, the choice to act or not to act is dependent on their intention to act. The intention to perform a behavior is the summation of three components: a person's attitude toward the behavior; the subjective norm; and the perceived behavioral control. Put more simply, choosing to act is based on a person's attitude toward the behavior, their perception of how others view the behavior, and their beliefs about their ability to complete the action. See Figure 3.1 for a graphical depiction of this interaction.

These factors are not necessarily evenly weighted by an individual, and in the case of handwashing, it is clear that a widely held belief (92%) that handwashing is a good thing outweighs the perception that others don't wash their hands and don't value handwashing, and that handwashing is difficult.[6] How do we know this? If it weren't so, the intention to wash their hands would be much lower than 80%.

So, why the lackluster 57% compliance rate with handwashing guidelines? Consider that a full 65% of physicians believe they do not actually know the guidelines for handwashing. When tested for guideline knowledge, 35% could not correctly answer four questions about handwashing. Even when physicians knew they were being watched, compliance rates only increased to 61%.[6] Physicians did not actually know how to be compliant with handwashing guidelines!

Like so many other attempts to engage physicians, handwashing has focused on disseminating the importance of handwashing instead of engaging physicians in accomplishing handwashing. Extrinsic measures, such as observation, are regularly used with disappointing results, while the way physicians learn is ignored. A new approach that meets physicians where they are is needed, or else critical patient needs will not be met for still

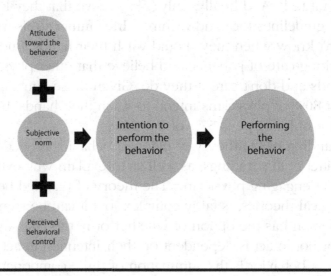

Figure 3.1   The theory of planned behavior.

another 200 years. That new approach is the focus of the remainder of this book, as we explore ways to affect the intention to perform a behavior.

There are few approaches that increase how positively someone feels about an action, increase their belief that others care about the action, and increase their belief that they can perform the action. However, there is one approach that accomplishes all three: positive deviance. Positive deviance is based on the observation that in every community, there are individuals who are able to be successful when others are not, due to their uncommon behaviors or strategies. Positive deviance is a systematic approach that identifies the successful but uncommon behaviors or strategies and then disseminates them across the community. The focus of positive deviance is identifying what is going right and amplifying it, as opposed to finding what is wrong and fixing it.

Positive deviance was first described in the early 1990s by Tufts University Professor Marian Zeitlin in her book *Positive Deviance in Nutrition.* In her book, she described the existence of children in poor communities with widespread malnutrition who were notably better nourished; she called these well-nourished children "positive deviants."[7] She was an advocate for identifying the behaviors of the positive deviants and using the lessons learned to address malnutrition in the community. Jerry Sternin learned about Professor Zeitlin's findings while he was a visiting scholar at Tufts University. He and his wife put Zeitlin's findings to the test to address malnutrition in Vietnam.

The year was 1991. Jerry Sternin was the director of Save the Children in Vietnam and was tasked by the Vietnamese government to develop a sustainable intervention that addressed malnutrition in rural villages where the childhood malnutrition rate was over 60%. Multiple interventions had had short-term success, but there were no sustainable solutions. Based on Zeitlin's ideas, the Sternins identified families whose children had managed to beat the odds and remain well nourished. The Sternins then invited the community to explore what those families were doing differently. Together, the Sternins and the community discovered that the families of the well-nourished children added tiny shrimp, crabs, and sweet potato greens to the children's meals and fed them four times a day instead of twice. All villagers had access to the shrimp and crabs in the rice paddy fields, but only a few used them in their children's food. Many families believed that adding the shrimp and crabs was bad for young children. The families of malnourished children were encouraged and taught how to prepare similar meals for their children. The program resulted in the successful treatment of several hundred malnourished children and the prevention of malnutrition for thousands of future children.[8]

The focus on positive deviance in the Vietnam malnutrition program tackled all three areas of the theory of planned behavior. First, perceived behavioral control was addressed by identifying families within the community that were successful in preventing malnutrition. These families were just like everyone else in the community, with the same access to resources for children's nutrition; everything these families did to nourish their children could be replicated in other families without additional resources or skills. Second, positive deviance addresses subjective norms. The villagers believed that malnutrition could not be prevented without outside resources and that shellfish was bad for children. The community-based discovery demonstrated that members of the community were able to prevent malnutrition and that families were feeding children shellfish safely. Finally, education and encouragement about collecting and preparing shellfish for meals increased the villagers' positive beliefs about the behavior, the third element of the theory of planned behavior. With all areas increasing, the intention to prevent malnutrition by including shellfish and sweet potato greens in children's meals also increased. Thus, the actual behavior increased, and children were less malnourished.

Since this initial field testing of the ideas, the process of using positive deviance has become more standardized. The simplicity of the approach, using observation, straightforward communication, and demonstration of success of people nearby, can easily be applied in the healthcare setting today. In one example, researchers at the Hospital Israelita Albert Einstein applied the methods of positive deviance in working to improve hand hygiene compliance. A basic tactic included sharing information at a routine meeting. "This meeting included healthcare workers (HCWs) from all shifts and gave these HCWs opportunities to express their feelings about hand hygiene, to discuss what needs to be improved, and to note good examples. Monthly [Hospital-Acquired Infection] rates were shown to the HCWs who worked in the intervention unit."[9] The meetings addressed participants' attitudes toward the behavior and their perception of how others viewed the behavior, and bolstered their beliefs about their ability to complete the action by noting how others had been capable of making improvements.

At the heart of physician engagement is applying the theory of planned behavior in whatever issue you are working on: address how good they feel about an issue, increase their belief that others care about the issue, and bolster their confidence that they can do something about it. For people whose jobs are often stressful, busy, and complex, having a clear line of sight to making a change for something they care about is actionable and desired. As long as they feel or think that the issue is not important, that the right people don't care about it, or that there's nothing that they can do about it, they won't engage. It's a pointless effort in a world where all the ounces of effort they can muster are already assigned to responsibilities. You have to make them prioritize the issue you are seeking engagement on by giving them the mind-set that it matters and is possible—and, importantly, that they personally can do something to make a difference.

References

1. Henry, J., Y. Pylypchuk, T. Searcy, and V. Patel. 2016. *Adoption of Electronic Health Record Systems among U.S. Non-Federal Acute Care Hospitals: 2008–2015.* ONC Data Brief 35. http://dashboard.healthit.gov/evaluations/data-briefs/non-federal-acute-care-hospital-ehr-adoption-2008-2015.php (Accessed July 1, 2016).
2. Centers for Disease Control and Prevention. 2013. *National and State Healthcare-Associated Infections Progress Report.* January 14, 2015. www.cdc.gov/hai/progress-report/index.html (Accessed July 1, 2016).
3. Pennsylvania Health Care Cost Containment Council. 2013. *Cardiac Surgery in Pennsylvania: Information about Hospitals and Cardiothoracic Surgeons. Data: July 1, 2011 to December 31, 2012.* www.phc4.org/reports/cabg/12/ (Accessed July 1, 2016).
4. Kolstad, J. T. 2013. *Information and Quality When Motivation Is Intrinsic: Evidence from Surgeon Report Cards.* Cambridge: National Bureau of Economic Research. www.nber.org/papers/w18804 (Accessed July 1, 2016).
5. Kaiser Family Foundation. 2015. *Aiming for Fewer Hospital U-Turns: The Medicare Hospital Readmission Reduction Program.* January 2015 Issue Brief.
6. Pittet, D., A. Simon, S. Hugonnet, C. L. Pessoa-Silva, V. Sauvan, and T. V. Perneger. 2004. Hand hygiene among physicians: Performance, beliefs, and perceptions. *Annals of Internal Medicine.* Vol. 141, 1, 1–8.
7. Zeitlin, M., H. Ghassemi, and M. Mansour. 1990. *Positive Deviance in Child Nutrition.* Tokyo, Japan: The United Nations University Press.
8. The Positive Deviance Initiative. *History.* www.positivedeviance.org/about_pdi/history.html (Accessed July 1, 2016).
9. Marra, A. R., L. R. Guastelli, C. M. Pereira de Arau'jo, J. L. Saraiva dos Santos, L. Carlos, R. Lamblet, M. Silva Jr, et al. 2010. Positive deviance: A new strategy for improving hand hygiene compliance. *Infection Control and Hospital Epidemiology.* Vol. 31, 1, 12–20.

Chapter 4

Achieving Shared Outcomes

Key Concepts

- Always seek to create shared outcomes.
- Four common unifying themes in healthcare are
  - Patient care.
  - Patient experience.
  - Financial stability.
  - Reputation.
- Engaging physicians requires active listening to understand the perspective of your physician partners so that you're in a position to suggest shared outcomes; without understanding their motivations and desires, you can't create an outcome that aligns with their goals.
- Effective communication with physicians is essential to engaging them in initiatives:
  - Listen actively.
  - Remain collaborative.
  - Seek to understand.
  - Find common ground.
  - Make the meeting easy on them logistically.

Thinking of financial compensation as the only way to motivate physicians is impractical and lazy.

Sometimes you are well prepared and have sufficient experience to accomplish the task you are assigned, but when you are in residency and fellowship, that is rarely the case. It is much more likely that you will be thrown into the deep end and expected to swim. The latter was definitely the case when I was tasked with leading an institution-wide sepsis improvement task force during my first year of fellowship.

I had spent over a year researching why our sepsis mortality rate was high and developing the analytical tools we needed to track our compliance with best practices. But developing subject expertise and creating tools did not create institutional improvement. For that, I needed to lead a large multi-disciplinary work group dedicated to changing how clinicians behaved. As a fellow, I had no authority to make anyone do anything and was, by default, considered inexperienced—which seemed appropriate given that I was still in training. The success of this task force would likely make or break my fellowship. With essentially no authority, I was left with only knowledge, tools, and influence. Success would mean tackling the problem of sepsis mortality from the ground up.

Step 1 was to assemble a team of nurses, physicians, pharmacists, administrators, and quality improvement personnel who agreed we had a problem, but didn't have enough authority to hijack the task force. Luckily, I was teamed up with an experienced quality improvement specialist, and we were able to quickly find an energetic, engaged group of like-minded professionals. This approach allowed us to tackle defining our problem quickly. We all agreed, in a decision that was considered very controversial, to use the new definition of sepsis as defined in the Surviving Sepsis Campaign.* This allowed us to address the care of a wider population, but went against the decades-old traditional definition. Essentially, the new definition included patients who were less sick. Our focus was on preventing those patients from getting sicker. It was the common vision of the group that if we could catch patients early in the development of their sepsis, we could stop it from getting worse and thus save lives. Over several months, the group developed protocols and designed education to teach clinicians how to identify sepsis early and then what to do when they did. Two primary metrics were identified: (1) the delivery of antibiotics

---

* See Society of Critical Care Medicine, Surviving Sepsis Campaign at www.survivingsepsis.org/.

within one hour of sepsis being identifiable and (2) preventing the development of organ damage, with the ultimate goal of reducing mortality in this patient population.

The task force was making amazing progress, and we were just a few weeks out from our implementation date when the medical director for the medical intensive care unit decided to attend one of our meetings. She was not someone who shared the group's vision, nor did she support of the new sepsis definition—and she had the authority to hijack the task force. Despite the headway we had made, she vehemently fought against our position, and as a unified group, we pushed back. The heated discussion ended in the predictable "Well I guess we can agree to disagree." Given the sink or swim nature of my position, I strongly countered, "No we can't. You can change the group's mind or we change your mind or we can vote, but we cannot disagree. We have to pick a direction." I'm not sure I had ever seen an attending physician that mad before. Without another word, she simply stood up and left. The task force did vote, and voted to stay with the original plan. The views of the group were greater than the opinions of one person with authority.

I did not know it at the time, but what the task force had just accomplished was creating a shared outcome. Shared outcomes are critically important for physician engagement, and they led to tremendous success with regard to the task force.

Achieving shared outcomes means establishing a common vision of the problem, the desired outcomes, and the indicators of success. A common vision is the most challenging part, since, in this context, *common* refers to belonging to the whole. Just think on that for a second: what this means is that achieving shared outcomes means defining a problem, describing desired outcomes, and defining indicators of success that everyone accepts and owns. When was the last time you were a part of a team that took the time to establish individual ownership of the problem, results, and metrics? I bet you have fond memories of that team. I also bet it was the exception, not the rule.

If you want to engage physicians, shared outcomes need to be standard practice. It is frequent that collaborators (administrators, nurses, pharmacists, financial specialists, and other healthcare workers) and physicians are in conflict with each other. Often, the physician's side isn't understood and valued, or the physicians overpower the other groups in decision-making. The remainder of this chapter will be dedicated to exploring how to establish shared outcomes with physicians by active listening to understand their concerns and needs while delivering potential solutions to address those concerns and needs in a manner that generates a robust collaboration rather than simply surrendering to the demands of the physician or agreeing to disagree.

Active listening is not as simple as just listening. It is a set of techniques used by negotiators and therapists to develop a mutual understanding in an empathetic environment. You can't force other people to practice active listening, but through leading by example, you can create a significantly more positive and impactful interaction. Multiple sources have slightly different definitions of active listening, so we will outline the approach that we have found effective.

TOOLKIT FOR ACTIVE LISTENING

1. Schedule a series of discussions. You are unlikely to reach mutual understanding in one meeting, and the expectation of this creates too much pressure. Plan to get together regularly over time. If the idea of more meetings is abhorrent, consider your priorities and decide whether this issue is important enough to replace other time commitments to create the space needed for face-to-face conversations.
2. Select a beneficial time and location to get together. Schedule the meetings around the physicians' clinical schedule, always showing deference to patient care commitments. Having a doctor run off to the operating room in the middle of a conversation won't help. Pick a location that is quiet, private, and conducive to an open and honest discussion. We encourage selecting a location that is comfortable to the physicians. They will be less defensive if they are in a familiar setting. No one responds well to being called into the principal's office. It will also increase the likelihood that they will attend.
3. Set an agenda and limit distractions. Put cell phones and tablets away. Take notes on paper. Ask the physician to do the same, except for pagers or cell phones (if that's how they are contacted for patient care issues). Let the physician know that you understand they may need to step away for patient care, but otherwise please put away any distractions. Set a good example here by demonstrating your commitment to a good conversation.
4. Use positive body language and make eye contact. Physicians are used to controlling the atmosphere of a room. If they feel the need to exert dominance, they will. Your presence needs to

communicate an openness to discussion and collaboration. Most physicians are keen observers of non-verbal communication, so be mindful of yours. In fact, because of the importance of non-verbal communication, we highly suggest that you avoid scheduling virtual meetings. Coming together in a shared space, with particular awareness of body language, will improve communication.

5. Don't use abbreviations, and freely ask physicians to clarify theirs. We learned this the hard way: when discussing comorbid conditions, we used the common abbreviation "CC." Our orthopedic surgeons were very confused about why we thought they could exert any control over car crashes. Don't assume that doctors are well versed in any hospital operating or financial terms or abbreviations.

6. Be prepared to educate. Physicians did not study healthcare operations or reimbursement methodologies in medical school or residency. Don't assume they know how the hospital or clinic gets paid or how supplies get to the operating room. For most physicians, healthcare operations are a mystery, a completely separate discipline managed by experts in other fields.

7. Listen attentively, and paraphrase your understanding. "I hear you saying … Am I understanding you correctly?" "Can you please go into more detail about … I am not sure I understand your perspective." In healthcare, seeking understanding often involves peeling back multiple layers to get to the core problem. It is essential to take the time to get to the core of the issue. We are frequently asked how we get physicians to come to meetings with us, and our answer is that we listen to them and demonstrate an understanding of their points by sharing back what we heard. Physicians find it a valuable use of their time to meet when the meeting yields understanding and progress.

8. Talk attentively. The physicians are much less likely to be attentively listening, so you must actively assess their receptiveness and understanding while you speak. After educating or giving your perspective about the topic at hand, be curious about their understanding. Ask, "Does that make sense?" "How do you see that fitting into what you just told me?" "Do you feel like we are coming from a similar space?" These kinds of questions feel uncomfortable at first, but they are the start of an open rapport with the

physicians. Also, purposely control your responses. If you get interrupted, you can't respond negatively or in kind. Instead, focus on
hearing what they're saying to figure out why they're getting impa-
tient and interrupting. Circle back to the tactics in Step 7 to assure
the physician that he or she is being heard, and that should calm
them down enough for them not to feel the need to interrupt.

9. Summarize both your and the physicians' perspective at the end of
the conversation, and write up a summary from the discussion so
that main points and action items are recorded and can be reviewed.
Physicians, like many of us, don't want to read long meeting minutes that arrive attached to an e-mail days after the meeting. If your
organization or personal style necessitates taking minutes, feel free
to create minutes. But communicate the high points and action items
succinctly to the physicians in an easily digestible short format that
does not require opening an attachment to increase the likelihood
that they—and other busy colleagues—will read the follow-up.

Sometimes, this process is fast; other times, it takes several meetings to
get going. It is often iterative. Achieving mutual understanding does not
mean you have reached agreement or a common vision of the problem. But
it does mean that you have mutually defined the starting point and have a
decent idea that you want to move in the same direction.

Moving from the starting point of mutual understanding to a common
definition of the problem is generally hard work. Your perspective and the
physician's perspective may seem to have little overlap. It is now your job to
merge the two by finding the unifying theme. Patient care and the patient
experience are frequently areas that can connect the perspectives, as are
financial stability and organizational reputation. There are other connectors,
but as previously discussed, if you can connect around the patient, you will
have the best success. It is, of course, why we are all here in healthcare.

For example, you meet with your surgeons about failure to document
a history and physical before the patient arrives in the peri-op area. After
completing several meetings, you believe that the surgeons understand your
concerns, but they have expressed that they don't see the problem with the
delays it causes, as they are frequently waiting for the right supplies to get to
the operating rooms anyway.

On the surface, surgeons not completing the history and physical before
patient arrival in peri-op does not seem to overlap with surgical supplies

delaying surgeries. However, using the patient as a connector leads to a common problem of "inefficient processes that delay surgeries and negatively impact the experience of patients." It is a shared problem: one that does not blame the physicians—nor does it give them a pass. They clearly have a role in inefficient processes and should be invested in a positive patient experience.

Now that you and the physicians have a common problem, you need a common vision of the ideal outcome. What started as a meeting to get physicians to document on time will now morph into a meeting about defining an efficient and patient-satisfying patient experience. We have found that this shift is almost palpable. The entire energy and dynamic of the group changes. Unlike the energy in defining a shared problem, all parties are interested in defining the ideal outcome, and everyone likes to give their opinion about how healthcare ought to be mananged. Start at the beginning of the problem and define what the patient should experience, what the finances should look like, what your reputation should be, or state any other goal. Gather the ideas from all parties to ensure that you're including goals from every perspective. Look for ways to combine multiple goals to draw in various parties, such as both nurses and doctors or both financial leaders and administrators.

Continuing with our example, the vision of the ideal outcome would be: when the patient arrives at peri-op, all paperwork is complete, they can immediately be prepped for surgery, all supplies are on hand, surgery can start on schedule, surgery ends when it is scheduled to end, the patient has no complications from surgery, and the patient's family is informed as the patient moves through the process. When casting the common vision, each group frequently provides more details and objectives than they initially brought to their definition of the problem. In our experience, this is not uncommon.

Once stakeholders are on the same page, collaborators and physicians can push for an ideal vision of outcomes. This is why, especially in healthcare, the process does not stop here. The groups must push through the next step as well: agreeing on shared indicators of success.

Defining common metrics is a significant challenge, and it is made even more difficult by an idealized vision of outcomes. This is where that vision clashes with reality. What can we realistically measure and track? What resources do we actually have? Which gap between the current state and the ideal state will be tackled first?

There will be many more questions as you settle on common indicators of success.

Remember, this isn't about assigning separate indicators to different groups, but establishing a definition of success owned by everyone involved.

Indicators should be straightforward to describe, using terms that stake-holders from all areas can easily understand. At the same time, no indicator should belong solely to an individual group. Indicators must be easily measured and reported, and tied to time-specific goals. These time lines are what separate shared *indicators* of success from the shared *vision* of success. The shared vision should be ultimately attainable, but in many aspects aspirational. The vision of success should be the ideal state, not an incremental improvement. The shared indicators of success are those incremental improvements. These improvements should be defined with achievable goals, on achievable short-term time lines.

Our example provides us with several common measures of success and several that are not. In traditional ways of thinking, problems defined by individual groups would translate to the indicator of success. The metrics would be the percentage of histories and physicals performed prior to patient arrival and the percentage of surgeries where all surgical instruments are available at the start of surgery. However, those are not common indicators; each is measuring something specific to a member of the group.

In our example, the shared indicator is surgeries starting on time. The shared metric is the percentage of surgeries that start on time. Because the indicator and the metrics are shared, this allows the groups to work together. This doesn't mean that you don't measure the other two indices to find opportunities for improvement; rather, it demonstrates that individually, they aren't an indicator of success.

Again, notification of patients' families and complication rates are not shared indicators. A common indicator in this case might be patient satisfaction. Improvement in the common indicators should be tied to time-dependent goals, that is, X% improvement in the next 3, 6, 12 months and so on. We will begin discussing how to use data to increase engagement and drive the desired improvement in the next chapter.

The creation of shared outcomes can drastically change the direction of a project to engage physicians. In the example, we moved from an administrative desire to improve compliance with timely documentation to a common goal of improving the timeliness of surgery and the patient's experience with surgery. The administration did not cave in on their goal of improved documentation, and the physicians did not give up their goal of improved surgical supplies management, but both are now engaged in delivering an improved experience for their patients. The dynamic changed from one of conflict and compromise to one of collaboration and goal setting.

Chapter 5

A Model for Physician Engagement

Key Concepts

- The Physician Engagement Maturity Model can help you frame up the steps to take in driving your organizational change initiative.
- Think of your change initiatives as having two main driving components: (1) using data-driven strategies to create actionable knowledge and (2) engaging physicians in a meaningful way.
- Creating actionable knowledge requires analytics to generate knowledge from your data and using a variety of knowledge-sharing tactics to effectively drive action.
- Physician engagement comprises three main aspects: fostering collaborative communications, developing shared outcomes, and defining and sharing metrics.
- Each of the components moves through stages, from little or no activity to an active and purposeful mastery of the domain.

After six months, the sepsis task force had done an excellent job of developing shared outcomes. We had a shared vision of the problem: mortality from sepsis was too high, and patients in the emergency department weren't getting consistent treatment fast enough. A positive outcome was seen as clinicians recognizing the signs of sepsis faster and a 33% reduction in mortality. Indicators of success included administration of antibiotics within one hour of arrival to the emergency department, reduced days in the intensive care unit, and reduced deaths.

The group knew that administration of antibiotics within 60 minutes of emergency department arrival was a lofty goal, but research indicated that mortality increased 70% for every hour antibiotics were delayed. "Lofty" might actually be an understatement. We had knowledge from historic analytics that compliance with the 60 minute metric was less than 5%. Thankfully, over the six months of working together, the group had developed an open collaboration. We took the knowledge of our poor compliance and an analysis of the emergency department's antibiotic use to the group. After reviewing the findings, one of the highly engaged pharmacists identified a major obstacle to meeting the metric. The most common antibiotic that was ordered for these patients had to be mixed in a sterile hood in the pharmacy, which took more than 30 minutes. To meet the 60 minute metric with that antibiotic, there were only 30 minutes to identify the patient with sepsis, order the antibiotic, run the antibiotic up from pharmacy, and have the nurse administer the medication. It simply was not realistic. This conclusion led to the creation of a new antibiotic algorithm that focused on selecting antibiotics that could be rapidly administered. Taking the time to select the "right" antibiotic was replaced by rapidly administering a reasonable antibiotic. The algorithms allowed for converting to the "right" antibiotic after the first dose was given. Executing the new algorithm required changing the hospital's formulary to purchase a self-stable antibiotic that could be administered as quickly as 5 minutes after being ordered, meaning that instead of having about 15 minutes after arrival to identify patients with sepsis to meet the 60 minute antibiotic metric, they now had around 55 minutes. Evidence indicated that the formulary change would save lives; however, it required physicians to switch mind-sets. They would have to change from working to select the best antibiotic (because decision-making takes time) to ordering an antibiotic that had a high probability of being effective while they gathered information for more decision-making. With the help of the task force and executive support, the practice and formulary changes were implemented. The time to administering antibiotics greatly improved, and more patients survived.

Moving from poor performance on a metric to formulary and practice changes that saved lives occurred because the task force was working at advanced stages of physician engagement. The efficiency and magnitude of these changes—mortality was reduced by over 25% within the first few weeks—led us to analyze the success of the team. That analysis produced the foundational concepts for the Physician Engagement Maturity Model discussed in this chapter.

The Physician Engagement Maturity Model (Figure 5.1) is designed to analyze and provide a framework for physician engagement strategies, not to comprehensively explore effective tactics. After this chapter, much of this book will focus on specific tactics to advance physician engagement. Here,

		Stage 1	Stage 2	Stage 3	Stage 4	Stage 5
Data-driven	Knowledge	No data sharing	Data sharing	Information sharing	Knowledge sharing	Sharing actionable knowledge
	Analytics	No analytics	Description analytics—historic	Description analytics—current	Predictive analytics	Prescriptive analytics
Engagement	Communication	No communication	Intermittent communication	Routine communication	Active communication	Collaborative communication
	Shared outcomes	No shared vision	Shared vision of the problem	Shared vision of the problem and outcomes	Shared vision of the problem, outcome and indicators of success	Actively evaluating shared indicators of success
	Metrics	No metrics	Reporting non-shared metrics	Reporting shared metrics	Evaluating shared metrics—historic	Evaluating shared metrics—real time

Figure 5.1   The Physician Engagement Maturity Model.

we will lay out the framework and discuss why each aspect and each step forward makes sense in driving physician engagement.

The maturity model is based on effective strategies within two domains: a Data-driven domain and an Engagement domain. The maturity stages are based on how physicians are motivated, learn new skills, and adopt innovations, and what is needed to develop shared outcomes with physicians. The two main domains are made up of five subdomains. The Data-driven subdomains are Knowledge and Analytics. The subdomains for Engagement are Communication, Shared Outcomes, and Metrics. As depicted in Figure 5.1, each subdomain ranges from Stage 1 (least advanced) to Stage 5 (most advanced). The stage of the main domain is the lowest stage of its subdomain, meaning that Analytics is a Stage 4, and Knowledge is a Stage 2, then Data-driven is a Stage 2.

Stages 1 through 5 exist on a spectrum where Stage 1 means little to no activity in a domain and Stage 5 represents an active and purposeful mastery of the domain. Frequently, projects that require engagement get out of balance, with a focus on a single subdomain, which leads to failed physician engagement and confused administrators/collaborators. For this reason, the overall maturity stage is based on the lowest subdomain stage. Therefore, it is necessary to understand the various stages of each subdomain.

The Data-driven domain is composed of Knowledge and Analytics subdomains. The Knowledge subdomain references the creation of in-depth understanding that drives action. Analytics involves the use of data to improve decision-making. Thus, the Data-driven domain is the use of data to improve decisions about which actions to take. At the most advanced stage, the decisions are so clear that the actions are automatically taken. The Knowledge subdomain is based on a knowledge management construct in which data is a collection of facts; information is facts placed in context; knowledge is a combination of multiple information streams; and actionable knowledge is a combination of information streams complete enough to make it clear what actions will be effective.

For example, Stage 1 of the Knowledge subdomain would mean having no data about hurricanes. Stage 2 is sharing that there are approximately 11 hurricanes annually in the Gulf of Mexico. Stage 3 is sharing that those 11 hurricanes occur primarily during the late summer and early fall. Stage 4 is knowing that tropical storms frequently become hurricanes; the current date is September 15; your location is the south Florida coast; and there is currently a tropical storm over the Bahamas that is likely to become a hurricane. Stage 5 is knowing, based on predictive models, that the likely hurricane will have landfall in south Florida, making the action of evacuation a straightforward decision.

Continuing with the hurricane-tracking example, let's explore the Analytics subdomain. Stage 1 indicates that no mathematical or statistical calculations have been performed on the available data: that is, that there are hurricanes in the Gulf of Mexico. Stage 2 is descriptive analytics of past events, such as averages, rates, counts, metrics, etc. In the hurricane example, it would be the calculation that on average there are 11 hurricanes annually. Stage 3 would be a description of a current tropical storm: where it is, how fast it is moving, and its past trajectory, as well as the current air and water temperatures. Predictive analytics, Stage 4, are probabilistic and machine learning techniques to forecast the likelihood of events/outcomes. For example, given the current description of the storm and environmental conditions, there is a 75% likelihood that the storm will become a hurricane, and based on predictive models about its trajectory, it is likely to hit land in Florida. Stage 5 is about creating a threshold of certainty that requires an action; that is, there is a 90% likelihood that a Category 5 hurricane will hit the south coast of Florida in 36–48 hours, so it is clear that an evacuation should be ordered.

Severe weather prediction is an excellent example to continue exploring the Engagement subdomain of communication. We couldn't imagine not communicating a pending natural disaster, but advance communication is limited in physician engagement. For severe weather, we have mobile phone applications, tornado sirens, flood warnings, that's 24 hours/day weather channels, and so on. For physician engagement, we might have monthly or quarterly reports and often no communication. Stage 1 is No Communication: the knowledge that administrators/collaborators have is never given to physicians. Stage 2 is Intermittent Communication, where knowledge is shared in a convenience model instead of in a scheduled manner. If/when the physicians are around, they get information. Stage 3 is scheduled and intentional communication of knowledge. Stage 4 builds on Stage 3, but leverages the active communication techniques discussed in the last chapter. The purpose is to ensure that physicians understand and contextualize the knowledge being provided. The most advanced stage is Collaborative Communication. This is where the focus is not only on providing the physicians with knowledge, but also on actively engaging the physicians to share their knowledge so that you can understand and contextualize their position as well. In the hurricane example, the spectrum would range from not notifying the inhabitants of Miami that a hurricane was coming, to providing evacuation updates every 30 minutes, to creating feedback loops so that citizens could notify authorities about traffic jams, downed trees, and flooding in evacuation routes.

The Shared Outcomes subdomain of Engagement is covered in detail in Chapter 4. With regard to the maturity model, Stage 1 represents no common ground: no shared vision of the problem, outcome, or indicators of success. Stages 2 through 4 move through the shared outcomes process of developing a shared definition of the problem, followed by a common definition of the desired outcomes, and finally, agreed-upon indicators of success. Stage 5 is active tracking of defined indicators of success.

The last subdomain of Engagement is Metrics. In this context, a metric is a measurement that describes a structure, process, or outcome. It must have a clear definition and a consistent method for measurement. Metrics are a subdomain of Engagement (rather than Data-driven), because when used effectively, they contribute significantly to communication and shared indicators of success. Stage 1 is having no metrics. Stage 2 is reporting metrics that were created by only one side of a partnership. This stage is common in healthcare because many governing/regulatory bodies impose metrics on healthcare institutions. Stage 3 is establishing metrics that all parties understand and agree to use. Stage 4 is analyzing historic metrics to identify opportunities for improvement by making changes to structures and processes. Stage 5 is analyzing real-time metrics in order to take immediate action that will improve the metrics and shared indicators of success.

Collaborators are often confused over why one initiative had high physician engagement and the next initiative, using the same tactics, had little to no physician engagement. In our experience, this is because the overall maturity needs to be at Stage 3 to generate good physician engagement. A single tactic or predetermined set of tactics will only intermittently advance the Physician Engagement Maturity Model to an overall Stage 3. To explore this further, let's examine two initiatives that require physician engagement. The first is the sepsis improvement program that we mentioned at the start of the chapter. The second is a program around hospital length of stay. Although both are inpatient examples, the lessons are directly transferable to ambulatory and other healthcare settings and situations.

WALKTHROUGH OF THE MATURITY
MODEL: THE SEPSIS TASK FORCE

Understanding how sepsis mortality was dramatically reduced in just a few weeks was the foundation for this maturity model. The team's serendipitous journey to an overall Stage 4 reveals the model's power. At the inception of the team, they were a Stage 1 in almost every subdomain. There was no data sharing, only some historic descriptive analytics, no communication, no shared vision, and no agreed-upon metrics. The initial meeting was the first time most of the team members were shown the historic analytics that suggested we had a mortality problem.

Over the course of 6 months, total absence of data sharing (Stage 1) progressed to reporting mortality and antibiotic use on a monthly basis (Stage 3), to discussions of antibiotic formularies and factors leading to sepsis deaths (Stage 4), and finally, to the determination that we needed formulary changes and to shift focus from the "right" antibiotic to an appropriate antibiotic administered quickly (Stage 5). You can see this progression notated in Figure 5.2. Analytics describing the historic rate and contributions to sepsis mortality (Stage 2) advanced to descriptions and visualization of current rates and contributing factors (Stage 3) to the ability to predict the impact on mortality of formulary and antibiotic algorithm changes (Stage 4). In the Engagement domain, all the subdomains started at a Stage 1. The organization had no communications about the issue of sepsis mortality, no shared vision of the problem or desired outcomes, and no sepsis-related metrics. The group moved quickly to routine communication about the task force's activity and the opportunity to improve sepsis care (Stage 3), to planned and active education about necessary changes (Stage 4), to open and bidirectional dialogues with physicians (Stage 5). The active and collaborative communication allowed the development of a shared vision of the problem and desired outcomes (Stage 3) as well as a progression to shared indicators of success (Stage 4) and the ability to evaluate those indicators as a group (Stage 5). The task force was able to take the shared indicators of success and use them to define metrics about sepsis treatment and outcomes, including time to antibiotic administration, number of days patients spent in the intensive care unit, and mortality rate (Stage 3), and those metrics were routinely reviewed during task force meetings (Stage 4).

The team's rapid progression through the model was key to its success. The team advanced through this model not by plan, but because we were all committed to helping patients, and the personalities of the group allowed a collaborative approach. More patients can be helped by using this model to proactively move initiatives forward when engagement is lacking.

In contrast to the serendipitous journey of the sepsis task force, tackling length of stay (LOS) was a very deliberate intervention. As is common in healthcare, hospital administration was sharing a multitude of information about LOS (Knowledge—Stage 3) and had descriptive analytics about current and historic LOS (Analytics—Stage 3) as well as frequent and active communication (Communication—Stage 4). However, there was no shared vision (Shared Outcomes—Stage 1) and only reporting of non-shared metrics (Metrics—Stage 2).

Being at a high stage of knowledge, analytics and communication took a lot of effort, and administration felt they were working hard but were not having success. They failed to realize that despite all their efforts, the physician engagement was an overall Stage 1. An initiative was started to change that engagement. We were able to reframe the problem from physicians not trying to discharge fast enough to patients staying too long. The focus became the shared vision that the best outcome was for patients to stay no longer than was expected for their medical condition. This shared vision was important, because it allowed a twofold path to address LOS. The first was to discharge a patient sooner, and the second was to create better documentation that justified a longer-than-anticipated LOS. The team then settled on one core indicator of success: no excess patient days. For the shared metric, excess patient days was defined as the number of days in the hospital above a risk-adjusted expected LOS. Active communication about physician

Overall Stage		Stage 1	Stage 2	Stage 3	Stage 4	Stage 5
		START			FINISH	FUTURE GOAL
Data-driven	Knowledge	No data sharing (start)	Data sharing	Information sharing (monthly mortality and antibiotic use reports)	Knowledge sharing (antibiotic formularies, factors contributing to sepsis deaths)	Sharing actionable knowledge (determined need for formulary change to facilitate rapid administration of antibiotics)
	Analytics	No Analytics	Description analytics—historic (start: historic rate and contributing to sepsis mortality)	Description analytics—current (descriptions and visualization of current rates and contributing factors)	Predictive analytics (predict the impact on mortality of formulary and antibiotic algorithm changes)	Prescriptive analytics
Engagement	Communication	No communication (Start)	Intermittent communication	Routine communication (routine communication about the task force's activity and the opportunity to improve sepsis care)	Active communication (planned and active education about necessary changes)	Collaborative communication (open and bidirectional dialogues with physicians)
	Shared outcomes	No shared vision (start)	Shared vision of the problem	Shared vision of the problem and outcomes (agreed-on definitions of sepsis)	Shared vision of the problem, outcome and indicators of success (defined door-to-antibiotic time as success)	Actively evaluating shared indicators of success (review mortality and door-to-antibiotic time at task force meetings)
	Metrics	No metrics (Start)	Reporting non-shared metrics	Reporting shared metrics (defined metrics: time to antibiotic administration, number of days patients spent in the intensive care unit, and mortality rate)	Evaluating shared metrics—Historic (metrics routinely reviewed during taskforce meetings)	Evaluating shared metrics—Real time

Figure 5.2 A walkthrough of the Maturity Model: The sepsis task force.

groups' excess patient days led to more collaborative physician communication, which, in turn, moved information sharing to knowledge sharing. This also allowed some simple predictive analytics about the potential impacts of process changes. The identification and use of a shared metric through the creation of a shared vision of the problem, outcome, and indicators of success advanced the overall stage of the model from a 1 to a 4 (Figure 5.3).

Not surprisingly, LOS began to fall. The best illustration of the impact of the project was a process change by the division of hematology. They had several hundred excess patient days and had been a focus for the LOS team for a long time. After being charged with reducing excess patient days, they presented a plan to tackle their problem. For convenience, they had almost all of their patients come to the hospital the night before inpatient chemotherapy started; no special care was delivered during that night, but it had been their standard practice for years. The division decided that they could change some of their workflows so that patients could arrive early in the morning on the day they were due to get chemotherapy, thereby eliminating one excess patient day for each of those patients. In all of the discussions about more rapid discharge or reducing LOS, they had never considered taking a day off at the front end. Once the change to early morning arrival was put in place, the hematology group's average LOS fell by more than half a day, and their excess patient days were greatly reduced. The group also worked hard to improve their documentation around how sick their patients were to improve the accuracy of their patients' expected LOS. Those two measures almost eliminated excess patient days for the hematology group.

The Physician Engagement Maturity Model is a road map for developing physician collaborations that drive successful interventions for patients and healthcare. In the midst of a struggling collaboration, determining which domains are at low stages clearly highlights where work needs to be done. With new collaborations, a focus on not allowing domains to get out of balance while ensuring they advance will lead to success. However, moving through these stages requires reflecting on what we know about how physicians learn and make decisions, how shared outcomes are developed, and the tactics to influence physicians effectively. The necessary tactics to positively collaborate with physicians and advance stages in the maturity model are the focus of the remainder of this book.

Overall Stage		Stage 1	Stage 2	Stage 3	Stage 4	Stage 5
		START			FINISH	FUTURE GOAL
Data-driven	Knowledge	No Data Sharing	Data sharing	Information sharing *(start: information about LOS)*	Knowledge sharing *(drivers for excess patient days)*	Sharing actionable knowledge *(Sharing most impactful process changes to reduce excess patient days)*
	Analytics	No Analytics	Description Analytics—Historic	Description analytics—Current *(start: descriptive analytics about current and historic LOS)*	Predictive analytics *(predictive analytics about potential impacts of process changes)*	Prescriptive analytics
	Communication	No communication	Intermittent communication	Routine communication	Active communication *(start: frequent and active communication from administration)*	Collaborative communication *(quarterly meetings with bidirectional dialogue about causes of excess patient days and interventions to reduce them)*
Engagement	Shared outcomes	No shared vision *(start)*	Shared Vision of the Problem *(patients staying too long)*	Shared vision of the problem and outcomes *(patients staying no longer than is expected for their medical condition)*	Shared Vision of the Problem, Outcome, and Indicators of Success *(patients staying no longer than is expected for their medical condition; success measured by no excess days)*	Actively Evaluating Shared Indicators of Success
	Metrics	No metrics	Reporting non-shared Metrics *(start)*	Reporting shared metrics *(reporting excess patient days)*	Evaluating shared metrics—Historic *(quarterly review of excess patient days by division and administration)*	Evaluating Shared Metrics - Real time

Figure 5.3   A walkthrough of the Maturity Model: Tackling LOS.

Chapter 6

Creating and Sharing Knowledge

Key Concepts

- Data analytics is about discovering the story you need to tell.
- Knowledge is required to drive action. Data alone without context is not influential.
- The creation of knowledge is separate from the sharing of knowledge. The work you do to review data, find the story, and understand the message is a separate activity from communicating your discovery.
- Use the blink test to evaluate whether your data visualization will be effective.

One of the most disheartening experiences when trying to create change within an organization is the moment you realize that you've lost your audience. Eyes gloss over, e-mail checking ensues. This scenario is common for people working with physicians: I've heard refrains of "They just won't listen" or "They only gave me five minutes and none of their attention." Presenting your case to physicians in a way that captures their attention and engages them as your partners requires careful attention to *how* your case is presented. Two aspects are critical here: (1) a clear problem statement and (2) a follow-up course of action.

Back in 2013, when the healthcare industry was reacting to a mandate to transition to the International Classification of Diseases 10th Revision (ICD-10) code set, Dr. Showalter and I were tasked with changing the documentation habits of 500 physicians to support the new requirements. Our solution was to engage the physicians in the overarching goal of "Clinical Documentation Excellence," which, as we defined it, transcended ICD-10 and served as a solution for all of the documentation requirements that physicians were struggling to understand in an era of healthcare reimbursement reform. After multiple discussions with physician and executive leadership, the University of Mississippi Medical Center agreed to adopt Clinical Documentation Excellence as an organizational goal. Physician leadership communicated that doctors were ready to do whatever needed to be done to achieve this "Excellence," and now the hard work fell to us to operationalize this response.

We brought together a multi-disciplinary team of physician revenue cycle specialists, hospital and professional fee coders, and clinical documentation improvement (CDI) nurses to identify documentation issues and solutions. These team members were adept at reviewing, analyzing, and highlighting instances in clinical documentation where physicians had left out an important detail, failed to clarify a critical point, or missed an element that could potentially impact patient care or reimbursement. Using a data-driven set of priorities, we asked the team to put together data about the documentation issues by physician specialty that could then be presented to our physician colleagues as a starting point for improving their documentation. Dozens of charts were reviewed, data on whether critical information was unclear or missing was collected, and charts were compiled in preparation for a meeting to engage the physicians. Dr. Showalter and I discussed the work with the team and were confident that the data was the right information to present. A meeting was set to address the problem statement: "Physicians within this specialty, your documentation lacks clarity and/or content that is needed to achieve Clinical Documentation Excellence." Physicians agreed to listen, and from their point of view, to be a part of identifying and employing a solution to our problem.

Primed as the physicians were to understand what they needed to fix, the conversation should have been a slam dunk. But that day, Dr. Showalter and I failed to ensure that the data was drawn up in a way that would work *for doctors*; it was instead formatted in a way that worked really well for CDI nurses and medical coders. Those health information management employees live in a world of written rules and regulations, doing most of their work on a computer reviewing other people's work. The tables of data they compiled were well organized, detailed, and comprehensive. Many elements that were tangential to the main point were included, as "further evidence" that the problems identified were part of larger patterns. The tables fitted the page, had row and column headers, and legitimately included data that supported the issue at hand (see Figure 6.1). What the tables did not do was communicate effectively the salient points, nor did they spur anyone to action. Instead, they overwhelmed with a mass of similar-looking data points all saying, "This is what's wrong" and nothing pointing to what we needed to change or how to create that change.

The conversation went something like this: 5 minutes of a CDI nurse explaining nine columns in three sections each with 20 data points, followed by the department chair of neurosurgery Dr. Louis Harkey putting his head in his hands and saying, "I can't make heads or tails of this." I knew I was in trouble when at 10 seconds in, Dr. Showalter had taken the data handout, flipped it over, and starting drawing a graph. We salvaged the conversation by thanking the team for all their hard work in unearthing examples and promising Dr. Harkey that we would reconvene with better information.

To move forward, we faced the question: How can we present this same information differently, so that instead of leaving confused and irritated at a waste of his time, Dr. Harkey walks out with a plan? This is the process

MS DRG MCC/CC capture rate- febrauary 2015 neurosurgery

Total visits		MCC/ or w/o MCC				CC/MCC or w/o CC/MCC				MCC or CC				All			
												MCC, CC or w/o CC					
DRG type	Total visits	MCC	w/o MCC	MCC capture rate	80% tile norm capture rate	CC/MCC	w/o CC/MCC	CC/MCC capture rate	80% tile norm capture rate	MCC	CC	MCC capture rate	80% tile norm capture rate	MCC or CC	w/o CC	MCC or CC capture rate	80% tile norm capture rate
Medical	14	0	2	0.00%	41.67%	0	0		78.26%	6	2	75.00%	48.20%	8	4	66.67%	84.58%
Surgical	51	3	3	50.00%	21.05%	1	0	100.00%	58.02%	16	13	55.17%	48.31%	29	15	65.91%	78.39%
--	65	3	5	37.50%	--	1	0	0.00%	--	22	15	59.46%	--	37	19	66.07%	--

MS DRG MCC/CC capture rate- march 2015 neurosurgery

Group		MCC/ or w/o MCC				CC/MCC or w/o CC/MCC				MCC or CC				All			
												MCC, CC or w/o CC					
DRG type	Total visits	MCC	w/o MCC	MCC capture rate	80% tile norm capture rate	CC/MCC	w/o CC/MCC	CC/MCC capture rate	80% tile norm capture rate	MCC	CC	MCC capture rate	80% tile norm capture rate	MCC or CC	w/o CC	MCC or CC capture rate	80% tile norm capture rate
Medical	22	2	3	40.00%	41.67%	1	0	100.00%	78.26%	6	4	60.00%	48.20%	10	6	62.50%	84.58%
Surgical	37	4	1	80.00%	21.05%	1	0	100.00%	58.02%	14	10	58.33%	45.31%	24	7	77.42%	78.39%
--	59	6	4	60.00%	--	2	0	0.00%	--	20	14	58.82%	--	34	13	72.34%	--

Figure 6.1   An example of great data with poor presentation.

of transforming data into actionable knowledge. The data has to tell a compelling story that leads the reader to take action. First, we figured out what message we were trying to convey and then cut out all details that were not critical to that focal point. Second, we thought about the data from our audience's perspective and found a metric that fitted with their priorities and understanding. Next, we changed the data from a table to a graph and removed the individual data points. And last, we added a goal line and color to indicate whether the data showed green (good progress—as in the "Base DRG Rate" graph at the top of Figure 6.2) or red (poor progress—as in the "Major DRG capture rate" on the bottom of Figure 6.2). To aid the discussion, we identified a few examples that would explain the graph if we were asked for more detail.

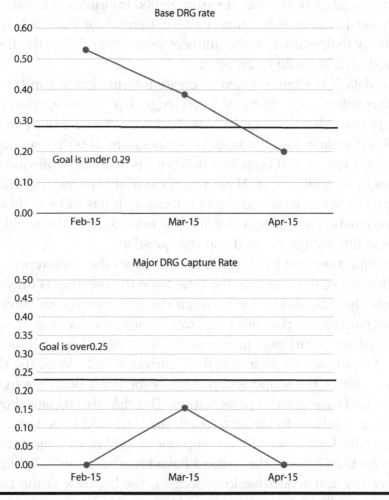

Figure 6.2   An example of great data with great presentation spurring action from knowledge.

The result was a much-improved conversation with Dr. Harkey that led to an amazing improvement of their metrics in the coming months. If I remember correctly, his comments after that second discussion were, "This information is compelling and I'm sorry I was slow on the uptake. We need to do something about this situation. But, never show me data like that other table again."

A great deal of work fails to result in demonstrable returns. The problem? The work focuses on collecting and creating data and information, neither of which drives action. *Knowledge* is required to drive action. Rather than creating data or information, valuable work creates knowledge, and that leads to action. So, what's the difference between data, information, knowledge, and actionable knowledge?

Data is isolated facts. This could be the time, temperature, heart rate, or any other number of discrete measurements. Information is data put into context. For instance, is the time Eastern, Central, or Pacific? Is the temperature a body temperature or the ambient temperature? Was the heart rate measured on a neonate or an adult?

Once data is put into context to create information, it can be combined with other information to create knowledge. For instance, noon in Tokyo occurs 13 hours before noon in New York City. While a body temperature of 90°F is definitely low, an ambient temperature of 90°F may be high or low. A heart rate of 130 bpm in a newborn is average, while a heart rate of 130 bpm in an adult is fast. However, none of this knowledge allows you to make a decision, let alone a good decision. It has to be combined with more information to create actionable knowledge. The threshold for reaching actionable knowledge depends on the question.

Some questions are easy: when do I dial into the conference call? You need the time of the meeting, the time zone the meeting is in, your time zone, and the time difference between the two time zones. Some questions are hard: is the patient's heart rate a cause for concern? You need the patient's current heart rate, their historic heart rate, their age, the normal values of heart rate for their age, their current activity level, the rhythm of their heart beats, the shape and pattern of the heart beats on an electrocardiogram, and their clinical presentation. The risk also dictates how much knowledge you have to create to reach the threshold of actionable knowledge. "Should I ask a set of follow-up questions?" needs significantly less knowledge than "should this patient have brain surgery?" The difference between data and actionable knowledge is the bedrock of the Data-driven domain of the Physician Engagement Maturity Model.

It is important to note that the *creation* of knowledge is separate from the *sharing* of knowledge. The Analytics subdomain described the range of knowledge creation from none to the *creation of actionable knowledge that is so clear the action should be automatic,* or prescriptive. The Knowledge subdomain is focused on sharing knowledge in a way that causes physicians to act. It ranges from *no data sharing* to *sharing actionable knowledge.* It is easy to see why sharing knowledge that is so clear physicians automatically react generates more engagement than sharing no data and not performing analytics, but the path between the two is not so easy. This chapter will provide you with tactics to navigate through the stages of data-driven maturity.

In any data-driven endeavor, the point is to make decisions and act according to data instead of anecdotes or impressions. This only works when data, information, and knowledge are shared in a motivational and digestible way. As described in the vignette that started this chapter, actionable knowledge will not drive action when it is shared in a way that confuses people. In our experience, there are dozens of ways to share knowledge incorrectly, and a narrow approach that is successful. Beyond simply encouraging you never to start with the rows and columns of a spreadsheet, we will concentrate on how to share knowledge well.

Clear communication of data, information, and knowledge is about creating easy-to-understand visuals. These visuals do not require fancy tools. Very successful visuals can be created in commonly used applications like Excel and PowerPoint. But, they must tell a story. We have received some very puzzled looks when we suggest this. The story does not have to be complicated, but it needs to be readily understood. For example, the value 8% does not tell a story. It could be good or bad; it could represent progress or failure. But with the right visual, even 8% can tell a story. Eight percent can be a green bar on a graph with a goal line drawn at 10% and text below that line that says our goal is to be under 10%. Now 8% tells a story. The story is that you set a goal of 10% and you are 2% beyond that goal. The story is that you are being successful. Or it could tell a story of failure. It could be a red bar on a graph with a line drawn at 3% with text above the line that reads our goal is to be under the line by 3%. Very quickly, you can move from sharing data to sharing knowledge by focusing on telling a story.

As noted above, the visual must be easily understood. Here are some guidelines to developing visuals that are easily understood.

TOOLKIT FOR DISPLAYING DATA TO CREATE ACTIONABLE KNOWLEDGE

- Use color to convey the message. Some colors, such as red and green, have meanings that are ingrained in our culture. Green is for things that are good, and red is for bad. Colors such as blue and black carry less innate meaning.
- Include a title or heading that is meaningful to your *audience*.
- Avoid abbreviations.
- Ensure that all your metrics and units are appropriately and clearly labeled.
- Choose a time period that is relevant. Data from 2 years ago is less meaningful than data from 2 days ago. This is more challenging than it sounds, since many publicly reported metrics run 1–2 years behind.
- Choose an appropriate scale. People, especially physicians, hate it when they are tricked by the scale on a visual. Making a minor gain or loss look big by changing the scale, or vice versa, almost always gets noticed and reduces trust.
- Remove any extraneous detail. If it distracts from the story, take it out.
- Make sure it passes the blink test.

What is the blink test? It is as straightforward as it sounds. Is your visual so clear that someone can almost instantaneously understand it? You can test it yourself, but it is generally better to have someone else test it. Have them close their eyes, pull up the visual on your screen, or hand them a printout. Then allow them to look at it for three seconds, or less, and close their eyes again. Ask them to tell you the story they got from the image. If they tell you the story you are trying to tell, it passes the blink test. If not, it doesn't.

Great visuals transform complex ideas and processes into concrete stories. Using concrete stories allows physicians to draw their own conclusions and determine for themselves that your argument is correct. Since physicians are trained to trust their own decision-making the most, great visuals set the stage for them to get engaged in whatever you are attempting to change.

Being ready to suggest the next step is critical to capturing the momentum you gained by effective knowledge sharing and to transform alignment into an active partnership. Chapter 8 will cover successfully communicating with physicians in more depth. However, with regard to knowledge sharing, the key to the discussion is a clear statement of position with data to back it up. Never exaggerate or embellish when you tell your story.

Before you can share a story, you have to discover it. The Analytics subdomain is about finding the story. The subdomain ranges from *no analytics* to *prescriptive analytics*. No analytics means you have no data with which to find and tell the story. Stage 2 is *descriptive analytics—historic*. Historical descriptive analytics is the story of where you have been. It is frequently biased by institutional memory and told more as a memoir than as an investigational report. The older the data is, the more likely it is to suffer from a revisionist interpretation. Despite the work that often goes into creating descriptive data about where you have been, it rarely generates knowledge that results in a return on investment.

The next stage is *descriptive analytics—real time*. This is the story about where you are. This is the stage where you begin to gain insights that drive action and generate a return. Real-time descriptive analytics does an excellent job of demonstrating variation in performance and identifying opportunities for improvement. Individuals and groups need to take that information and put it in context to make decisions and take action.

Predictive analytics, Stage 4, tells the story of where you are going or where you might go. Predictive analytics can generate future visioning data, information, or knowledge. Predictive analytics that generates knowledge becomes a "choose your own adventure" story. It creates a level of understanding that lets you select the action that should take you to where you want to be.

Stage 5 is *prescriptive analytics*. Prescriptive analytics is the story of what you should do. It is the result of creating a story so persuasive that the necessary action is clear. Writing these stories has spawned an entire industry of informatics and analytics; there are many vendors who are skilled at this genre of storytelling. However, while some predictive and prescriptive techniques do require special skills to tell the story, there are some doable approaches everyone can take.

Practically speaking, we don't encourage you to spend much time developing historic descriptive analytics, even though there are times when it is your only option—you can't make the Centers for Medicare and Medicaid Service publish data more often. Real-time descriptive analytics is more effective, but not always possible to obtain. How do you determine whether you are generating real-time or historic analytics? It's not always clear. The time frame between real time and historic can get blurred. As a rule of thumb, anything over three months old is historic. Defining real time can be challenging. Some metrics require time to pass, such as 30 day readmission rates. The original event is 30 days old before you can even start the data-collection process. Gathering and publishing data are rarely done immediately, and effective knowledge sharing may take a few weeks. It may be that 45–50 days is the closest to real time you can accomplish. Other metrics, such as percentage occupancy, may be only a few minutes old.

Whether one year, two months or two minutes old, the data should be accurate, be useful to the physician, and be distributed regularly. Three types of visualization will meet the vast majority of your descriptive analytics needs: bar graphs, run charts, and scatter plots. Respectively, they show comparisons, progress over time, and correlation. These are the key storytelling techniques for descriptive analytics, whether they are real time or historic.

Let's return to looking at handwashing compliance. Bar graphs will show comparisons between compliance for physicians, nurses, and housekeeping, or between hospital units. One of the biggest visualization mistakes we see is using bar graphs of multiple groups over time. This is confusing. Bar graphs should be used for comparison over a single time period. Run charts should be used when a time sequence is needed. The compliance for each of 12 months can be compared between groups using a run chart. It will make the distribution easy to understand, and the progress between groups can be compared. For both bar graphs and run charts, goal lines are helpful to indicate success/failure. Arrows and text notes indicating interventions/changes can give a quick explanation for changes in the data. In this example, there could be an arrow that denotes that a new hand hygiene campaign was launched in January. It would then be clear that the gain after January correlated with the start of the program. Correlations are a great way to move data to knowledge. Timing correlations, like starting a new initiative, are best shown in run charts. However, correlations between two sets of data or information are best shown with a scatter plot. For example, you can compare hand hygiene with nosocomial infection rates. Scatter plots can then be divided into four quadrants. Quadrant I is where both the x and y axes are positive; in Quadrant II, x is negative and y is positive; in Quadrant III, x and y are negative; and in Quadrant IV, x is positive and y is negative. The quadrant cutoffs can be made based on group averages or institutional goals. The meaning of the quadrants varies by analysis, but they are excellent when you are trying to tell the story that good behavior leads to good outcomes and poor behavior to bad outcomes.

Infographics and advanced visualizations should be used when your primary tools fail to pass the blink test. There are many options when it comes to infographics and advanced visualizations, but they need to meet one of two standards. Either they need to pass the blink test or they need to be so engaging that the physician takes the time to digest the story. Infographics are designed to improve cognition by improving the individual's ability to recognize patterns and trends through the use of visual cues. Essentially, they work by turning data, information, and knowledge into pictures; the most effective infographics engage the visual processing system with commonly recognized symbols and patterns. They take advantage of color and iconography to rapidly communicate meaning. For instance, relative cost might be shown by changing the size of a dollar sign, or using a syringe or pill to represent different routes of delivery of a medication. Advanced visualizations are more about explicitly displaying patterns. They are frequently complex and fail the blink test. The patterns they reveal can uncover unknown relationships and previously undefined clusters. To be used with physicians, the visualization must be compelling enough to hold their attention while intelligible enough that the physicians can draw their own conclusions. Physicians are unlikely to tell you they don't understand your graph. Advanced visualizations are best used for communicating novel insights to physicians after you have reached advanced stages in the Engagement domain.

Predictive analytics is a collection of techniques that identify the chance of future outcomes based on the data, information, and knowledge available today. We are not going to discuss the actual techniques of predictive analytics; the techniques are too vast and varied to cover in this text. However, it is essential to understand that predictive analytics can create data, information, or knowledge. To illustrate this point, we will compare forecasting with simulation. Forecasting is simple: the prediction of a future event. Forecasting can create data or information, but usually not knowledge. When meteorologists predict rain tomorrow, they are delivering data by stating the likelihood of rain and information by telling you the likelihood at different times of day. However, you need to interpret that information based on your context to take action. Do you have a long walk from your parking space? Yes. You need an umbrella. No, because you park in a garage. You don't need an umbrella. Simulation, at least in predictive analytics, is designed to address various conditions and project likely outcomes. The use of simulations creates the ability to answer "what-if"-type questions. It is the basis for "choose your own adventure" storytelling. Since the predictions are placed in multiple different contexts, a great deal of knowledge can be generated. You can demonstrate which intervention is the most likely to be effective; which one will have the highest return on investment; and which ones may fail. Using predictive analytics typically requires working with a partner who has mastered the skills necessary to do the calculations. It is not necessary that you understand all the math to leverage predictive analytics, but you do need to understand the input, the assumptions, and the results. Physicians will not listen if you present the results and can't speak to how they were determined.

Prescriptive analytics builds on the "choose your own adventure" story-telling. When the "what-if" scenarios and possible outcomes present a choice so compelling that there is only one right course of action, you have prescriptive analytics. The most challenging part of prescriptive analytics is determining the threshold where action is clear. Taking action always has a cost. It may be an actual cost, such as using a more expensive piece of equipment, or it may be an opportunity cost, because you only have the ability to take one action. The cost has to be weighed against the benefit. Determining when to automatically act requires excellent engagement from physicians.

Chapter 7

Communicating Effectively with Physicians

Key Concepts

- Physician engagement requires active communication, meaning that you purposefully seek the understanding of the other party during discussions.
- Collaborative communication occurs when each side actively seeks the understanding of the other with the intention of achieving a common goal.
- There are six distinct tactics to address technology adoption based on the level of engagement and the challenges you face:
  - Facilitated innovation
  - Facilitated dissemination
  - Facilitated discovery
  - Directed dissemination
  - Directed discovery
  - Forced compliance
- To initiate engagement, start with communication aimed at seeking an understanding of the physicians' interest and involvement. After you have a productive dialogue, you can move on to defining shared outcomes and then finally evaluating shared metrics to determine success.

Car crash and major car crash. That was not what I expected to hear when I asked for his understanding of CC and MCC. From a hospital billing perspective, CC and MCC are complication or comorbidity and major complication or comorbidity. However, when we asked our orthopedic surgeons what they thought these abbreviations meant, they answered, "car crash" and "major car crash." This kind of disconnect is common when communicating with physicians. With knowledge of the disconnect, I was able to educate the physicians and advance our collaboration. I focused on treating them as just people and not some unapproachable class of superhumans.

Fixing this communication problem didn't fix all of our issues: the next time we met, we had even greater problems with our communications. The purpose of the meeting was to review questions about the documentation (queries) that the clinical documentation improvement (CDI) specialists were sending to the physicians. The physicians did not personally value the benefit of responding to the queries, and they found the queries confusing, so they were not sure what their responses should be. As a result, the queries were frequently ignored. The meeting almost immediately went downhill. Difficult-to-understand queries were passed out to the group, and the CDI specialist began to dive in. "Based on the coding clinic from 1994, subsection C, you must document the comorbid conditions by indicating …." The head of orthopedic trauma surgery leaded over to me and said, "I don't understand anything she is saying."

At that point, I interrupted the meeting and said, "Hey everyone, this is Matt. Matt is just a guy. He doesn't know what a Coding Clinic is and he isn't familiar with the list of comorbid conditions. Can you rephrase and just talk to us like you're explaining it to your mom or someone who hasn't been in healthcare?" The CDI specialist relaxed a little and started to explain the query in lay terminology anyone could understand. Once the surgeons understood what was being requested, they helped guide revising the questions so that anyone could get what they were after. The physicians thought this activity was worth their time, because as a teaching facility, they have the responsibility to train the residents, and the surgeons recognized that these queries provided a teaching opportunity. It took several more meetings, but eventually the new queries were written in a compliant, but clear and more simplistic format that made sense to both the physicians and the CDI specialist. The response rates dramatically improved, and the number of queries went down over time, as the physicians began to simply write the correct thing in the first place, negating the need for a query. The teaching aspect that the physicians liked, combined with the easy-to-respond-to format, gained the shared outcomes and vision that everyone wanted.

Engaging physicians is about creating a unified vision and working to achieve the vision. As described in our Physician Engagement Maturity Model, the Engagement domain consists of three subdomains: Communication, Shared Outcomes, and Metrics (Figure 7.1). Chapter 4 is dedicated to the creation of shared outcomes; the focus of this chapter will be the Communication and Metrics subdomains. As described in the vignette at the start of this chapter, communication is about more than having meetings. It is about establishing an active and open dialogue with common terms and common goals. The Metrics subdomain involves the creation and evaluation of common measurements. It is less about the data and calculations and more about tracking the success of a common vision.

		Stage 1	Stage 2	Stage 3	Stage 4	Stage 5
Data-driven	Knowledge	No data sharing	Data sharing	Information sharing	Knowledge sharing	Sharing actionable knowledge
	Analytics	No analytics	Description analytics—historic	Description analytics—current	Predictive analytics	Prescriptive analytics
Engagement	Communication	No communication	Intermittent communication	Routine communication	Active communication	Collaborative communication
	Shared outcomes	No shared vision	Shared vision of the problem	Shared vision of the problem and outcomes	Shared vision of the problem, outcome, and indicators of success	Actively evaluating shared indicators of success
	Metrics	No metrics	Reporting non-shared metrics	Reporting shared metrics	Evaluating shared metrics—historic	Evaluating shared metrics—real time

Figure 7.1 The Physician Engagement Maturity Model as seen in Chapter 5.

The Engagement subdomains are intentionally listed in the order Communication, Shared Outcomes, and Metrics. Engagement needs to happen in this order. First, you must communicate effectively with physicians; then, you need to define shared outcomes; and finally, you need to evaluate the shared metrics that track the success of the shared outcomes. Engagement is very difficult when you start with the metrics and work backward. But this is exactly how many incentive programs are established. A governing body or payer chooses the metrics and the incentives and then informs the physicians. As our model indicates, this results in poor physician engagement. The metrics are not shared, the communication is intermittent, and at best, they can achieve a shared vision of the problem. The result is a Stage 1 or 2 in the Engagement domain. Not surprisingly, most hospitals are struggling with the shift from volume to value as outside entities are creating the definition of value.

The tactics needed to establish collaborative communication are covered in Chapter 4. However, we would like to explore the Communication subdomain in the context of the transition to value. Stage 1 is no communication, or wholly ineffective communication. Sending out a transition to value newsletter that the physicians don't read doesn't count as routine communication. Hosting a town hall that very few physicians attend also doesn't count. For the purpose of the maturity model, communication only counts if it is bidirectional. However, bidirectional does not mean active or collaborative. Active communication involves purposefully seeking the understanding of the other party, and collaborative communication occurs when each side is actively seeking the understanding of the other with the intention of achieving a common goal.

In order for communication to be bidirectional, you must provide the opportunity and encourage physicians to ask questions and get clarification. Bidirectional communication requires in-person or virtual meetings. Current telecommunication technology removes the need for groups to be in the same physical location to have a two-way conversation. However, generating discussion in virtual situations can be complicated, and we encourage in-person meetings whenever possible. As a rule of thumb, bidirectional communication is occurring when one side is asking clarifying questions while the other is presenting.

The line between Stages 2 and 3, intermittent and routine communication, may be difficult to identify. However, we assert that intermittent communication occurs as part of other meetings at defined times, monthly, quarterly, biannual, and so on. Important updates are held until the predetermined time. Routine communication occurs as often as is needed to keep physicians up to date on items that impact the group's shared vision. This may be achieved with frequent meetings or the ability to bring the group together in an ad hoc manner. Intermittent communication typically uses pre-established challenges to disseminate broad information. Routine communication often uses narrow messaging in a targeted manner. For example, intermittent communication might present total pressure ulcer rates at a quarterly staff meeting, whereas routine communication would also include physician/practice specific pressure ulcer rates at biannual productivity reviews.

Stage 4, Active Communication, is all in the approach and is controlled by the presenter. However, in our model, Routine Communication must be reached before a group can progress to Active Communication. Active communication is the result of routine communication in which the presenter is practicing both active listening and attentive talking (described in Chapter 4). The presenter is seeking to understand what the physician is understanding and is striving to ensure physician clarity; this creates the basis for collaborative communication. Collaborative communication occurs when physicians are fully engaged in the conversation, actively listening and seeking their own understanding. This requires a common vocabulary, a common problem, and a common goal. Collaborative communication only occurs after the Shared Outcomes subdomain advances to higher levels. Physicians and collaborators must have a common definition of the problem, outcomes, and indicators of success to achieve collaborative communication.

Many health systems are attempting to transition to value while their Communication and Shared Outcome subdomains are at Stage 2. These are systems sharing the financial impact of the value-based purchasing programs annually and presenting hospital-acquired condition data at quarterly staff meetings. They are sharing data based on payer definitions; often, the data is only for a small segment of the whole patient population. The data is neither timely nor directly relevant to the physician. Health systems functioning at Stage 4 in both of the subdomains would be presenting physician-level information in a variety of settings. The information would be based on the physician's entire patient population, and indicators of success would have been agreed on by the physician and the hospital. The shared indicators may have definitions similar to the payers' definition, or may be broader. For example, the payers' definition of a pressure ulcer may exclude patients with a specific comorbidity, but the shared indicator might include all pressure ulcers without regard for comorbidities. The shared indicator should be something that drives results in the value model, but will frequently lack program exclusions. By determining the shared indicators of success, we drive the creation of meaningful metrics.

Metrics are certainly better than no metrics, but ownership of the metric determines how effective it is at engaging physicians. Significant effort is spent on creating and gathering metrics that physicians don't own. We categorize these metrics as Non-shared Metrics. Without a sense of ownership, even the best knowledge around a metric will create only limited engagement. Shared Metrics are the result of Shared Indicators of Success. This is where a number of highly resourced improvement activities fail. They never get past Stage 2 in metrics; thus, overall engagement remains at Stage 2. Engaging metrics are the result of well-executed Shared Outcomes.

Stages 3 through 5 are based on how well the group are using their shared metrics. Simply presenting the metrics to physicians is Stage 3. Stage 4 is the reporting and evaluating of historic metrics. Evaluating metrics requires active communication. The physicians need to add their perspective to the information generated by the metrics. They need to take part in root cause analysis and identifying opportunities for improvement. As discussed in Chapter 6, it can be difficult to determine whether you are evaluating a historic or a real-time metric. Generally speaking, if the data is over three months old, it is historic. However, even data that is only a week old can be historic, based on the metric. Stage 5 is evaluating shared metrics in real time. This might mean reviewing all pressure ulcers the day after they were identified, or information on readmissions every month. The closer in time the evaluation is to the event, the greater is the chance that the evaluation will be accurate. Lapses in time increase the likelihood of bias entering the evaluation.

Regardless of the engagement stage, it is necessary to consider adoption rates in communication. Communication tactics need to evolve as a behavior moves through the adoption curve, which we discussed in Chapter 2. Tactics that are effective for increasing adoption are markedly different depending on whether you are early or late on the adoption curve (Figure 7.2). However, we rarely see groups change their tactics. To address this issue, we have established six distinct tactics based on the level of successful adoption:

■ Facilitated innovation
■ Facilitated dissemination
■ Facilitated discovery
■ Directed dissemination

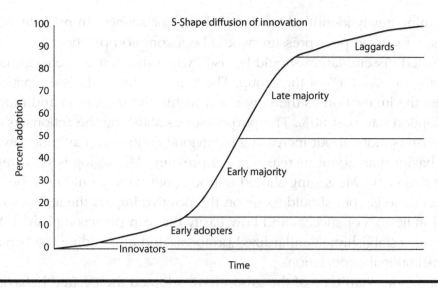

Figure 7.2   The diffusion of innovation curve with adoption groups.

- Directed discovery
- Forced compliance

Facilitated innovation is necessary when the desired behavior is not occurring at all, or occurring in fewer than 2.5% of the group. It represents techniques that involve group problem-solving to improve outcomes. Brainstorming is used to identify barriers, and innovators are encouraged to incorporate novel solutions from their diverse social networks. Communication focuses on increasing perceived behavioral control. It is challenging to get people to believe something is possible when no one is doing it. Casting a clear vision is essential.

Facilitated dissemination uses opinion leaders to develop consensus on the problem, the need for a solution, and acceptability of the solution identified by the innovators. It should be used when the desired behavior is occurring in 2.5%–16% of the group. Again, the purpose is to increase the group's perceived behavioral control. Communication should focus on the ability of the desired behavior to advance shared indicators of success; the outcomes often speak for themselves with this group.

When the desired behavior is occurring in 16%–50% of the group, the best tactic is facilitated discovery. Early adopters need to communicate their acceptance of desired behavior to improve the group's attitude toward the behavior as well as increasing peer pressure in the group. However, since physicians are convergent learners, the primary focus needs to be overcoming newly identified barriers to behavior change. In non-physician groups, a focus on peer pressure would be a common practice.

Directed dissemination should be used when the desired behavior is occurring in 50%–84% of the group. The focus of directed dissemination is to show the innovation as the new norm within the institution and move the adoption rate past 80%. The purpose of establishing the actions as the new norm is more about increasing behavioral control and attitude toward the behavior than about increasing peer pressure. Messaging is very important in this tactic. Messaging should not be about "you should do it because everyone else is," but should focus on the positive impact the action has on shared indicators of success and how easily that can be accomplished. We encourage establishing standardized protocols and embedding the behaviors into institutional expectations.

When more than 84% of the group have adopted the desired behavior, we recommend directed discovery. These techniques use small group/individual problem-solving sessions to overcome individual barriers or resistance to adoption. At this point, the assumption is that the physician would perform the behavior if he/she was able to and knew how. The group is afraid of failure. Communication and support need to focus on ensuring success and reducing anxiety. Once barriers are determined, elbow-to-elbow support may be needed to facilitate behavior change.

The final tactic is forced compliance. Even with the best engagement, there will likely still be one or two physicians who refuse to adopt a new practice. At this point, you need to determine how important 100% compliance is to your initiative. These physicians will not change unless they are forced to. These severe tactics can be used to motivate the final line of resistance and may include loss of hospital privileges or sanctions.

In the end, it is important to treat physicians as smart, but not omniscient, people who are looking for clear, concise communication that enables them to do something about issues they care about. Looking back to the theory of planned behavior, we know that a person's attitude toward the behavior; whether others care about the issue; and whether the physician believes they can make a difference all factor into their response. Craft your communications to combine their adoption group with the planned behaviors to understand your audience, and you will be well on your way to communicating effectively with physicians.

Chapter 8

Working with Physician Executives

Key Concepts

- There are four questions that can aid you in refining your approach to a physician executive:
  - Does the physician have a history of representing the physicians to the organization or a history of representing the organization to the providers?
  - Does the physician's position require making decisions across a single physician specialty, multiple physician specialties, or a diverse set of healthcare disciplines?
  - Does this issue deal directly with the executive's clinical experience?
  - Can I tie this decision to a concrete example from the physician executive's medical practice?
- There are four primary tactics to use to engage and influence physician executives:
  - Brainstorming/visioning to generate new ideas
  - Presentation of data/research to create reflection
  - Leveraging personal experience to drive understanding
  - Using opinion leaders/peers to expand perspectives
- By understanding the physician executive you're dealing with by answering the first four questions, you can select the strongest tactic for engaging with that executive.

It can be challenging to successfully communicate with physician executives. They are a self-selecting subset of doctors who require a distinct approach to communication. The group is divided into two subgroups: hospital/health system executives and ambulatory/practice leaders. Understanding which subgroup the physician executive is in has significant impact on how you should communicate. Complicating the situation further, health system versus practice is more of an approach or mentality than a role defined by position. Physicians in leadership roles in a health system can be primarily concerned with the impact their decisions have on the health system or with the impact on physician practice. The same holds true for practice leaders. The line between the two will continue to blur with new value-based programs and bundled payments. This blurring causes many people to take a middle-of-the-road approach with communication. We discourage such an approach and advise that you develop two distinct messages—one for physician executives with a health systems mind-set and one for physician executives with a practice-based approach.

Physician decision-making is affected by transitioning into leadership roles. They need to make decisions for groups instead of for themselves, and they need to make decisions about things they will not be able to experience. Frequently, business decisions will need to be made about problems outside of physicians' core training, such as nurse staffing models or selecting an outsourced billing group. These factors force physician executives to adapt their learning style and move toward the center on Kolb's learning styles (see Chapter 1 for more information on Kolb's learning styles). They spend more time and effort learning from peers and more time and effort reflecting on research and data presented to them. However, they still remain fiercely independent decision-makers and greatly trust their own opinion. The result is that physician executives will seek input from their peers and available resources, but will come to their own conclusion and not get swept along with the crowd. Many change initiatives have gained momentum with the chief financial officer (CFO), chief executive officer (CEO), chief operating officer (COO), and/or chief nursing officer (CNO), only to be stopped because the chief medical officer or chief of staff was not supportive. Achieving physician engagement by circumventing physician executives is unlikely to work.

Actively engaging the physician executive requires you to think through several questions. First, does the physician have a history of representing the physicians to the organization or a history of representing the organization to the providers? Does the position require making decisions across a single specialty, multiple specialties, or multiple disciplines? Does this issue deal directly with the executive's clinical experience? Can I tie this decision to a concrete example from the physician executive's medical practice? The answers to these questions help you identify which tactics are more or less likely to be persuasive.

Let's explore each question in more depth. Does the physician have a history of representing the physicians to the organization or a history of representing the organization to the providers? The answer to this question determines which mind-set/mentality the physician leader has: is he/she a system leader or a practice leader? It is important to note that there is no judgment in this answer. One is not better than the other, but decision-making between the groups is significantly different. In reality, physician executives exist on a spectrum between the two extremes, but for clarity we will treat them as separate groups. Physician executives with a health system focus are influenced by the good of the many. They will work hard to change the behavior of physicians if they believe it will lead to a clear return on investment for the health system. They are less concerned about whether there is a clear return for the physicians themselves or the physician practice (see Chapter 10 for a detailed discussion). They tend to be mission driven and highly persuasive leaders, since they often have to achieve physician behavior change that is against a physician's individual interest. Physician executives with a physician practice mind-set are more interested in achieving a return on investment for the physicians and their practices. They are less likely to make decisions that go against physicians' individual interests. These leaders tend to invoke loyalty from the physicians they represent and can leverage that loyalty to create behavior change. As with all physician decision-making, patient care is a trump card. Both leadership styles will support changes with clear benefits for patients.

Does the position require making decisions across a single specialty, multiple specialties, or multiple disciplines? This question defines how far outside of a physician executive's comfort zone he/she needs to reach to form an opinion or make a decision. If the leadership position is one where they are representing their specialty, such as managing partnering for a neurosurgery practice, they have personal experience with the impact of most decisions. In these cases, the physician will have little change to their learning style as they develop decision-making skills. When they need to make decisions for multiple specialties, such as a partner in a multi-specialty practice, they will be able to draw less on personal experience and will need to gather input from colleagues. When learning to make decisions in these roles, physicians will be pulled slightly toward the center of Kolb's model. However, decision-making will still be based on their personal experiences and those of the physicians they go to for advice/input. Physician executives who need to make decisions that affect multiple disciplines, such as health system chief medical officers or physician CEOs, will not be successful if they continue to rely on a convergent learning style. They must adapt. They have to consider the impact and input from other disciplines, such as nursing and pharmacy. They will take time to reflect on best practices and seek to understand the success of others. Those who are successful pull from the other learning styles and become centralist in their decision-making. Of important note, the newer a physician is to this type of position, the more likely they are to still rely on a convergent approach. This is also true for a physician who seems to be struggling in a system leadership position.

Does this issue deal directly with the executive's clinical experience? When the answer to this question is yes, you can basically throw out the answers to the first two questions. If you are dealing directly with a decision that involves or directly affects a physician executive's clinical practice, they will make a decision based on their experience. Peer input and reflection will have minimal influence. You will need to directly address their experience to influence the decision. We will cover how to do this later in the chapter. If the answer to the question is no, the executive will be more open to hearing other people's perspectives.

Finally, you must ask yourself whether you can tie this decision to a concrete example from the physician executive practice. This question is about choosing tactics. Physicians, even successful system-level executives, spent years learning to adopt new skills through personal hands-on experiences and are more comfortable making decisions when they have a personal frame of reference. Tying a personal and concrete example to a physician executive's decision-making can be a double-edged sword, so just because you can, this doesn't mean you should. Choosing the right tactic can be complicated, but making the right selection can greatly enhance your ability to influence the decision-making of physician executives.

We cannot offer you a foolproof guide to choosing the right tactics, but it has been our experience that using the four questions we described above provides a framework for increasing your odds of positively engaging a physician executive. Whenever possible, involve physician executives early in defining shared outcomes (Chapter 4). By involving them early, you will be able to incorporate their thoughts and ideas into the shared outcome and its metrics. Unfortunately, it will not always be possible to involve them. There will also be times when you need to engage them prior to identifying shared outcomes. When you engage physician executives outside of a shared outcomes model, lead with patient benefits. Many times, a decision doesn't directly impact patient care, and that's when the framework helps most.

Before applying the framework, it is necessary to review the tactics. Tactics fall into one of four main categories:

1. Brainstorming/visioning to generate new ideas
2. Presenting data/research to create reflection
3. Leveraging personal experience to drive understanding
4. Using opinion leaders/peers to expand perspectives

Brainstorming has not been a successful tactic for us. However, visioning has frequently been helpful. Visioning is done by asking the executive for their wish list or ideal state: simple questions such as, "Ideally how would you like to see this done?" or "If you could change one thing, what would it be?" Visioning can be a high-risk tactic. Only use it when you have a good idea of their ideal state and know that you can make changes that will move in that direction. The risk of using visioning is greatly reduced if shared outcomes have already been established.

Presenting data/research to generate thoughtful reflection is a very common tactic, but it is frequently low yield. Most people don't take the time to connect the data or research to intrinsic motivators. Remember, intrinsic motivation has been demonstrated to be four times more powerful than extrinsic motivation (Chapter 3). Whenever possible, tie the data/research to improvement and show the physician executive where the practice, hospital, health system, etc. ranks. For physicians, knowing that the group is doing poorly, or holds a leadership position, is a powerful intrinsic motivator.

No tactic is as powerful, or as perilous, as leveraging a physician's personal experience. Once this tactic is used, the physician executive will hold a strong opinion. That opinion may or may not be the one you are hoping for. Unless you have a long history with the executive, it can be difficult to predict what opinion may develop when you use phrases such as, "I'm sure you had a similar experience when you were treating patients." It is always best to reference a very specific instance that you are familiar with and believe you know the physician's opinion about; although that circumstance is rare unless you frequently care for patients with the executive. Due to the risk, we would like to advise you to avoid this tactic, but we can't. In some scenarios, it is the best, and sometimes the only, tactic to drive decision-making.

Expanding a physician executive's perspective with opinion leaders and peers is the safest of all the tactics, assuming you know what the person is going to say to them. This tactic is most effective when the physician executive is out of their comfort zone and has little personal experience with the decision that needs to be made. The intrinsic motivation for the physicians is that they want to help make a good decision for the group, and the extrinsic motivation is that they don't want to be seen making a bad decision. This alignment of intrinsic and extrinsic motivation means that the physician executive is open to thoughtful insights from individuals he or she believes are better informed and have had more personal experience. Opinion leaders and peers are markedly less effective when physician executives have their own experiences to influence their decision-making.

Now, let's explore how the four questions you should ask yourself interact with the four types of tactics (Figure 8.1). There is a lot of gray when choosing a tactic to engage a physician executive, but there are a few straightforward choices. Visioning is the right tactic when the executive is organizationally oriented and the decision involves multiple disciplines and does not directly deal with their specialty. In these decisions, the physician executive is not directly affected and has minimal barriers to helping cast a vision of the ideal state. They will trust disciplines closer to the decision to

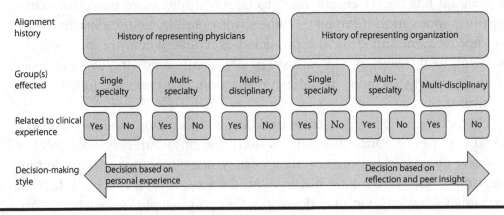

Figure 8.1 Physician executive decision-making style.

work out the details. Additionally, there is likely little research about what is most effective in multiple-discipline decisions. Given their passion for patient care, physicians are frequently idealistic when casting a vision, and you will probably need to inject some realism into the discussion. Vision is best done with all parties affected by the decision.

Presentation of data/research is most effective when the physician executive is organizationally oriented, the decision affects a single or multiple specialties, and it does not directly affect, and can be concretely tied to, the executive's clinical work. In this scenario, the decision affects physicians but not the executive. There is likely a body of research to guide the decision-making, and the executive will have a frame of reference, but no personal experience, to interpret that literature. The leaders of the multiple specialties may have conflicting opinions, which will limit the value of peer input and visioning. It is important to note that when presenting data/research, it is best to avoid pressing for an immediate decision. Schedule time for a one-on-one review of the research and a follow-up meeting in about a week to allow for reflection on what you presented. Be prepared for the physician to find his/her own research and to want to discuss how it fits in with what you presented.

As noted previously in the chapter, leveraging a physician executive's personal experience is the most powerful and perilous tactic. It is the best option when the executive is provider-oriented and the decision affects a single specialty, deals directly with their clinical experience, and can be tied concretely to an example from their medical practice. Frequently, they will initiate these discussions with a phrase such as, "Last week when I was on service …". These situations are also generated through quality improvement and risk management projects. When these scenarios present themselves, you have little choice and must dig into the physician's personal experience. The executive will likely have already formed an opinion. If that opinion is in line with the views of the other executives, you can simply help flesh out how to generalize the executive's vision. If it is in opposition, you will need to gather enough information to sway the other executives, sway the physician executive, or at very least make the physician feel that their position is understood.

Using opinion leaders and peers is most effective when the executive is provider oriented, the decision affects multiple specialties or disciplines, and it does not directly affect, but can be concretely tied to, the executive's clinical work. In this scenario, the physician executive wants to make the best decision for the providers and knows their opinion will be highly relied on. However, they don't have personal experience to bring to the table. They will be open to hearing from others who have been successful or whose opinion holds sway with the providers. The primary goal is to make a good decision. The secondary goal is to make a defensible decision. Being able to say, "Let's use X hospital (or specialty, etc.) as a model since they have been very successful" is highly defensible.

Real-life decisions rarely fall cleanly into a perfect tactic. Most often, multiple tactics are needed, and the benefits and risks of each must be considered. To explore this further, let's look at the scenario when a Chief Nursing Officer (CNO) is trying to persuade a physician executive to support decreasing the nurse staffing ratio (number of patients per nurse) from 6:1 to 4:1. Superficially, this looks as if it just affects nursing. However, the plan involves increasing nursing staff by 50%. Such a sizable expense generates considerable opportunity costs. Making the change will eliminate funds for several quality improvement positions, equipment replacements, raises, and additional physical therapists. How the CNO approaches the executive will clearly affect the support she receives.

The nurse staffing decision does not fit any of the clear tactical choices we have described, because it is a multiple disciplinary decision of which the physician executive will have direct patient care experience *and* that can be concretely tied to his/her own experiences, since the executive will have working relationships with the nurses. How does the CNO choose the best tactic? We recommend using our framework and choosing the tactic(s) with the most + values (Figure 8.2). There will likely be multiple tactics that are close, and we encourage using a balance of these. To demonstrate this, we will look at how the tactics score for an organizational-oriented versus a provider-oriented executive (Figure 8.3).

The provider-oriented executive has a clear tactic that will be most effective, leveraging personal experience. If there is a known event when the physician felt the negative impacts of the 6:1 staffing ratio, there is a clear communication strategy. The CNO can speak with the executive and say, "Remember a few weeks ago when you were upset with being put on hold while you waited for the nurse to pick up the phone and you were concerned the delay had almost harmed your patient? I think I have a fix for that. I would like to change the nursing staff ratio from 6:1 to 4:1. I foresee that addressing your concern. Can I work with your assistant to set up a time to do a call with the CNO and CMO from hospital X? I think it would help if you heard about their success." In that short conversation, the CNO

		Brainstorming/ Visioning	Presentation of data/ research	Leveraging personal experience	Using opinion leaders/peers
Does the physician have a history of representing the physicians to the organization or a history of representing the organization to the providers?	Organization	+	+	−	−
	Providers	−	−	+	+
Does the position require making decisions across a single specialty, multiple specialties, or multiple disciplines?	Single specialty	−	+	+	−
	Multiple specialties	−	+	−	+
	Multiple disciplines	+	+	−	+
Does this issue deal directly with the executive's clinical experience?	Yes	−	+	+	−
	No	+	+	−	−
Can I tie this decision to a concrete example from the physician executive's medical practice?	Yes	−	−	+	−
	No	−	−	−	+

Figure 8.2 Assessment questions and tactics.

touched on a negative personal experience, evoked visioning experience, and laid the foundation for opinion leader/peer influence. Those tactics would not have been as effective with the operationally oriented executive. The operationally oriented executive would also relate to the use of the negative experience. However, a transition to outsider influence would not have strongly influenced their position. A better tactic would have been for the CNO to say, "Remember a few weeks ago when you were upset with being put on hold while you waited for the nurse to pick up the phone and you were concerned the delay had almost harmed your patient? I think I have a fix for that. I would like to change the nursing staff ratio from 6:1 to 4:1. I foresee that addressing your concern and having many other positive effects. Can I work with your assistant to set up a time to meet with you and discuss how it could improve our hospital?" It is worth noting that neither type of executive is expected to be heavily influenced by data and published research. This is one more reason why establishing shared outcomes is essential for physician engagement.

We don't want to mislead you with our framework; it is not a precise prescription to physician executive influence. Communicating with physician executives is an art, and each individual will have nuances in how they make decisions, learn, and communicate. However, the framework does

	Organizationally-Oriented Physician Executive				Provider-Oriented Executive			
	Brainstorming/ Visioning	Presentation of Data/ Research	Leveraging Personal Experience	Using Opinion Leaders/ Peers	Brainstorming/ Visioning	Presentation of Data/ Research	Leveraging Personal Experience	Using Opinion Leaders/ Peers
Orientation	+	+	-	-	-	-	+	+
Multiple Disciplines	+	-	-	+	+	-	-	+
Direct Clinical Experience	-	-	+	-	-	-	+	-
Concrete Examples	-	-	+	-	-	-	+	-
Total +	2	1	2	1	1	0	3	2

Figure 8.3 Nursing staff ratio example. The scenario involves multiple disciplines and deals directly with concrete experience of the physician executive.

provide a collection of tactics that can be leveraged to improve communication, as well as questions to assess the issue that needs to be communicated. Mastering the skill of using these tactics and accurately assessing an issue are critical for physician engagement, because effective communication is the best way to engage a physician executive.

Chapter 9

Act Continuously for Sustained Engagement

Key Concepts

- Long-term engagement requires continuous effort over time. Participants should continuously ACT:
  - Analyze data to create actionable knowledge.
  - Collaborate to determine best actions.
  - Take action and tackle barriers.
- Efforts to create change while physicians are still in the early stages of the maturity model will be frustrating and likely ineffective, as the physicians are not positioned to listen and understand.
- Factors in assessing potential solutions include:
  - Barriers to successfully taking action.
  - Effort in taking action.
  - Likely impact of taking action.
- Long-term engagement is action oriented and requires administrators/ collaborators to be mindful of what increases the likelihood that physicians will take actions that support the long-term goals.

There is nothing more frustrating than declaring victory, only to watch your gains erode over 2–3 months, except maybe doing it again and again and again. That frustration was the start of my fellowship in Clinical Informatics and my attempts to lead data-driven change. Whether it was signing verbal orders, seeing patients endure urinary catheter-associated infections, intravenous catheter-associated bloodstream infections or nosocomial blood clots, the sharing of the data and opportunities for improvement would result in rapid improvements that would degrade over several months. As soon as we declared victory or shifted focus to the next problem, rates of negative events would increase. We would then circle back, and the cycle would continue. Some projects made slow, but steady, gains. But for most projects, we just chased our tails.

My first experience with this frustration was when I was working as a physician analyst right after medical school. The hospital had just gone live with computerized physician order entry, and verbal orders were being used more frequently than the institution wanted. The use of verbal orders was seen as a sign of poor workflow or inappropriate use of nurse resources. I was quickly able to write a report to identify that well over 50% of our verbal orders were coming from only 10 physicians. I worked with our physician champions to share this data with the target physicians and their leadership. The champions tackled workflow and education barriers with the problematic doctors. Within a few weeks, the number of verbal orders had greatly decreased, and the team moved on to other implementation problems. It was several weeks before I thought about verbal orders again. When I checked the numbers, they were almost back at baseline! I notified the champions, and they circled back to the physicians. The number of verbal orders improved again, so we started reporting the numbers monthly to help stabilize the improvement through monitoring and awareness.

During those times where gains disappeared, there was a lot of discussion about the Hawthorne effect. The Hawthorne effect is the change in people's behavior when they know they are part of an experiment. It commonly, and controversially, gets used to describe the gains seen from improvement projects that erode after the project is finished. The conclusion from discussions of the Hawthorne effect is to use the observer effect to your benefit:

report more data at more places, make observers more noticeable, and increase communication. Make the intervention group even more aware that they are still part of an "experiment."

Considering what we know about physicians, though, we can recognize that the "watch and report" approach will not work long-term with doctors. Extrinsic motivation will not change culture. Long-term clinical improvement requires physicians to change, and the culture and environment to change with them. Understanding that change requires looking more closely at the Hawthorne effect and why it is the bane of physician engagement.

The Hawthorne effect is the conclusion of an analysis of factory production studies done between 1924 and 1932 at the Western Electric factory in Hawthorne, Illinois. The experiments were overseen by Elton Mayo, a professor of industrial research at Harvard. The goal of these experiments was to determine which environmental factors—lighting, incentives, breaks, and so on—would result in the highest productivity. The Great Depression brought an end to the experiments and spawned multiple publications about industrial management. The experiments were immortalized by Henry A. Landsberger in 1958 when he published *Hawthorne Revisited*. His analysis indicated that the workers increased productivity every time the lighting was changed. Landsberger concluded that the workers knew they were being observed each time the variable was changed; thus, they felt important and worked harder. The most controversial aspect of the conclusion is that the observations made the workers feel *important*.

Study subjects may change their behavior due to observation (the observer effect) or due to the demands placed on them (the demand effect); this has become a stable consideration in experimental designs. Subsequent analysis of the Hawthorne data, published in 2011 by economists Steven D. Levitt and John A. List, calls into question whether the Hawthorne effect even played a role in the results seen in the Landsberger analysis.[1] Today, the Hawthorne effect is part of the healthcare improvement lexicon, describing the short-term improvement that often occurs when clinicians are made aware of an improvement project.

Hawthorne effect or not, there is a well-understood reason for these short-term changes in clinician behavior. After a request to modify actions, clinicians intend to act in accordance with the performance improvement project, because it is important to the institution. Declaring activities to be part of an improvement project communicates their importance to administrators and increases the subjective norm for the clinician. If you recall, in Chapter 3, we discussed the theory of planned behavior, which describes how increasing a person's view of the importance of an action to someone else (subjective norm) increases the likelihood that they will take that action. When the institution declares victory or moves to the next project, the subjective norm reverts to baseline, and so do the actions of the clinicians. Note that the improvements due to changes in subjective norm are frequently less dramatic with physicians, because as convergent learners, they are less influenced by what is important to others.

Physicians are more impacted by the other two factors in the theory of planned behavior: attitudes toward the behavior and perceived behavioral control. They are influenced to change their behavior based on their own opinions about a behavior and their belief that they can perform the desired behavior. Preventing the erosion of improvement and creating additional gains is about maintaining engagement over time. Maintaining engagement over time means taking physicians from "I didn't know that was important to you; this is not important to me and this seems hard," to "I know this is important to you; this is important to me and I know how to do this." Long-term engagement is about data-driven collaborative cultural change. We believe that long-term engagement is distinctive from iterative improvement cycles such as Plan-Do-Study-Act. Long-term engagement is about creating continuous pressure to improve through collaborative decision-making and mutual action. The result is a new culture: one where the actions of administrators and clinicians are emblematic of a shared vision.

Achieving this culture is hard, dedicated work and requires both groups to *Continuously ACT:*

- *Analyze* data to create actionable knowledge
- *Collaborate* to determine best actions
- *Take* action and tackle barriers

Long-term engagement cannot be successful at low stages of the Physician Engagement Model. Attempts are extremely frustrating for both collaborators and physicians. In fact, this is why the "observe and report back" approach described earlier is ineffective: this places Communication and Knowledge at Stage 3 of the Maturity Model, but Metrics revert to Stage 2, leaving the overall maturity at Stage 2 (see Chapter 5). The greatest long-term success will only be achieved when the overall maturity of the project reaches and maintains Stage 4 or beyond. When the initial excitement of the project is winding down, and competing priorities are reducing attendance at meetings, how do you morph from this waning project team to a program that leads both administrators and physicians to Continuously ACT?

How do you analyze data to create actionable knowledge? The first step is to focus on communication. Your success will hinge on achieving Stage 5 in communication. Long-term engagement means a collaboration, with each side contributing their knowledge and understanding of the problem and visions of success. The focus of collaborative communication needs to be on continually identifying barriers to and opportunities for achieving the shared indicators of success.

This is why shared indicators of success are critical to Continuously ACT. Without a clear understanding of how success is defined for a project, it is next to impossible to create actionable knowledge. When collaborative communication is continuously occurring, shared outcomes can advance to Stage 5, where physicians and collaborators are actively evaluating the achievement of these shared indicators of success. Evaluating these shared measures allows each side to share their perceptions, examine the data, and determine whether their perceptions are in line with objective measures; when short-term shared goals are met (or not), actionable knowledge is needed to advance the project. (More information about creating share indicators of success is available in Chapter 4.)

Therefore, once you have established collaborative communication evaluating shared indicators, the next step is to use those shared indicators to create knowledge—preferably actionable knowledge. You can create actionable knowledge from descriptive analytics with current data; predictive analytics is not essential to long-term engagement. Your focus should be on creating current descriptive analytics about the newly defined shared indicators of success to get the ball rolling. The information created can then be put into context by the group. Open, active, and collaborative discussion about the information is the foundation that will lead to new insights. Those insights are knowledge. They will give you an idea about what needs to be done. Most groups stop at this point, excited by their success in reaching this level.

To be a true change agent and achieve long-term success, you need to push past this and ask the hard questions about what exactly needs to change. What problem are you trying to solve? You get there by collaborative communication about how these new insights are helping you achieve your shared indicators of success or how they are preventing you from achieving them. This actionable knowledge will define actions that need to be taken and barriers to overcome. You want to keep pushing the group until you have a list of actions and barriers. This process of communicating collaboratively about shared indicators of success to identify barriers and opportunities for action, as supported by the use of descriptive analytics, is how you analyze data to create actionable knowledge.

After several months of working to prevent hospital-acquired blood clots, we had not yet reached our target shared indicators of success. We had hoped to have a greater than 10% reduction in occurrence in the first 6 months. While reviewing the data at our monthly meeting, it became clear that our education efforts had not led to consistent and appropriate risk stratification of our patients. We knew through a study of residents that they were better able to risk stratify patients after attending the education; however, they still were not sufficiently accurate to provide optimal care. Discussions with residents made it clear that they were unable to describe the nuances of risk stratifying patients despite the education, and thus did not know which prophylactic treatment to order. Armed with the knowledge that residents weren't able to optimally treat patients despite education improving their understanding, the group developed a number of potential actions: simplify the risk-stratification process; publish paper tools to guide risk stratification; develop an automated scoring system in the electronic health record; create a risk-stratification job aid within the electronic health record; and provide more intense targeted education.

Next, you must collaborate to determine the best actions. If you are at Stage 4 with analytics, predictive analytics can help. Predicting the impact of taking an action or removing a barrier allows you to prioritize interventions based on those most likely to have the greatest impact. As shown in the vignette at the beginning of the chapter, the group is likely to develop multiple potential actions. Each action will have its own benefits and challenges. When choosing the best action, the group must consider:

- Barriers to successfully taking action
- Effort in taking action
- Likely impact of taking action

It is an easy choice when one of the actions has no barriers, takes little effort, and will have a large impact. However, those easy, impactful actions are the unicorns of physician engagement. They are so magical, we aren't sure they truly exist. Almost always, you need to balance barriers, effort, and impact.

Barriers fall into four main categories: people, process, technology, and culture. Each element must be considered for each potential action. *People* barriers are based around resource constraints and needed skill sets. The main questions are: Do we have enough people to do this? Do we have the right people to do this? Do our people have the skills to do this? *Process* barriers represent difficulty with standard work. The main questions are: Do our people know what to do? Will it be difficult for our people to do this? Can we standardize what our people are doing to achieve this? Do we have the equipment/supplies for our people to do this? *Technology* barriers are software, hardware, and access issues. The main questions are: Do we have the right software to do this? Is the software optimally configured to do this? Do we have the right hardware to support this? Is the hardware optimally deployed to do this? Do the end users have access to what they need to do this? *Cultural* barriers include practice differences, language/terminology differences, organizational receptiveness to change and accountability, and the role of individual biases in allowing the group to create change. The main questions include: Are practices consistent enough to do this? Can we effectively communicate how to do this? Will the organization support us doing this? Will people be held accountable to do this?

We use *effort* in a broader sense than just man-hours. It is too difficult to split out the financial cost and resources from the human effort, and thus we combine them. When determining effort, you need to consider equipment/supplies, human capital, technology purchases, and the level of necessary approvals. The costs of equipment, supplies, and technology are the easiest to determine and translate to a hard dollar figure. Human capital is more tricky. There are straightforward man-hour calculations, but there are also opportunity costs to consider. If a person is working on this action, he/she isn't doing something else. The effort to get an action approved by an organization can be the most difficult to determine. Getting changes approved frequently intersects with institutional politics, and the effort can be unpredictable. The main items that have to be determined are: how much will this cost in terms of equipment, supplies, and technology; how many man-hours will go into this action; what else won't get accomplished if efforts are put into this action; how hard do we think it will be to get this approved?

Impact can generally be determined in one of two ways. The first is the group's best guess—and unless you have Mr. Spock in your group, this will likely not be accurate. The second is to use predictive analytics to calculate a likely return. The more basic your algorithm, the more likely it is to be wrong, but it should be better than a guess. The most basic prediction is based on how others performed when they made similar changes. Whether you found the intervention in the literature or from a presentation, you can predict based on the results of others. For example, you might use the sepsis improvement publication mentioned in Chapters 4 and 5 to predict that your similar sepsis intervention would lead to a 25%–30% reduction in risk-adjusted mortality. You might hedge and say you don't think you'll perform as well as the published result, but that it is reasonable to expect a more moderate 15%–20% reduction. A more advanced algorithm may be based on the outcomes for patients who received ideal care. In that case, you can predict the outcome if more patients received ideal care. For example, if patients have zero negative events with ideal care and one event for every 100 patients who receive less than ideal care, you can predict one fewer event for every additional 100 patients who receive ideal care. Advanced statistical and machine learning algorithms can yield even more precise predictions about the impact of an action.

The group must collaboratively explore the barriers, effort, and impact of purposed actions. The members must weigh and balance the pros and cons of each and come to a joint conclusion about which is the best action or actions to take. We recommend ranking those that can be done quickly near the top. The quick wins can be implemented while you put effort into the more challenging actions.

Five potential actions were considered by the group: simplify the risk-stratification process, publish paper tools to guide risk stratification, develop an automated scoring system in the electronic health record, create a risk-stratification job aid within the electronic health record, and provide more intense targeted education. Simplifying the risk-stratification process had cultural barriers; changing the risk-stratification process, even to make it more simple, wasn't best practice, and it went against what we had just trained. Additionally, it would be a high-effort intervention, requiring the retraining of all the residents, *and* we were unsure that it would have a positive impact. Publishing paper tools to guide risk stratification had few barriers; an educational sheet had already been created, and the residents were trained on the scoring system. The effort was low, since the educational sheet simply needed to be reformatted to a pocket card, printed, and distributed. We guessed that it would have a small, but positive, impact. Developing an automated scoring system in the electronic health record had technology and process barriers: not all of the information needed to do a proper risk stratification was available in the electronic health record. Building the scoring system was a significant effort, requiring a substantial amount of development by the electronic health record team and a considerable amount of validation by clinicians. The impact was unclear, given the likely inaccuracy of an automated algorithm based on incomplete data. Creating a risk-stratification job aid within the electronic health record had a process barrier: would clinicians accept and use the tool? Further, the tool would need to integrate into existing workflows. The effort was significant, requiring considerable development by the electronic health records team and auditing by clinicians. The impact was projected to be significant, because the rate of blood clots dramatically decreased when patients were accurately risk stratified and given appropriate prophylaxis. More intense targeted education had people and process barriers, namely, scheduling resident and attending time for education. The effort would be minimal, since the curriculum was already designed, but the impact was thought to be limited, given that only targeted areas would be affected.

The group eliminated an automated scoring system and simplifying the risk-stratification process due to the high barriers and effort. The group ranked the creation of pocket-sized job aids at the top of the list, with targeted education second. The creation of a job aid in the electronic health record to guide residents in accurate risk stratification and appropriate ordering of prophylaxis was ranked third due to its high effort, even though it was predicted to have the highest impact.

Finally, you must take action and tackle barriers. The group needs to create a plan to execute the top-ranked action(s). The plan may be as simple as creating an action list with deadlines or as complicated as a fully developed project plan. However, it must be written and communicated between group members, and all parties need to hold each other accountable for the execution of assigned tasks. Many groups falter at this point. Taking action means being an agent of change, which means paying attention to the deliverables and deadlines. The members of the group need to work together to support the organization through their planned changes, identifying means for staying on track. These can be as straightforward as creating a shared calendar that allows deadlines to be tracked and reminders set, or as complicated as having a formal project manager who oversees the work and makes sure that all members of the group are keeping up with their tasks and due dates. The group should decide how detailed they want to be in this effort, which means evaluating the impact and effort just as when selecting the objectives for their response. Do what works for your situation, but be sure to identify a way to track whether the project plan is staying on track and achieving its predefined metrics for success.

The group worked with the institution's print shop to create a pocket card explaining the risk-stratification process and suggested prophylaxis. During the rollout of the card, the lead physician performed targeted education with groups most likely to impact patient outcomes. While these interventions took place, the team worked with the electronic health record analyst to develop, build, and implement an electronic job aid that fitted into existing workflows. The job aid guided the residents through risk stratification and prophylaxis selection at the time of admission. Several training sessions were held to allow the residents to see how they would be interacting with the system. The implementation of the electronic aid occurred several weeks after the pocket cards had been implemented. The combination of interventions led to a greater than 15% decrease in hospital-acquired blood clots.

There are books and books about how to take action and tackle barriers. We will not attempt to do a comprehensive review of the topic. However, it is important to highlight the uniqueness of taking action and removing barriers while maintaining physician engagement. As previously discussed, physicians learn by doing, and all change requires learning. This means that physician engagement requires doing—and doing as close to the real thing as possible. A collaborative discussion may be enough for many administrators to have a clear vision of the change, but it will not be enough for most physicians. A hands-on experience that approximates the change will markedly increase a physician's belief about being able to complete a new behavior. For many physicians, the only thing that will convince them that they can do a new behavior is actually doing it.

The best example we have of this is simulated patient visits prior to implementing an electronic health record. We were working with a high-volume ophthalmology office that served an at-risk population and wanted to get their clinic back up to volume as soon as possible. To fully engage the physicians, we set up a simulated clinic in the evening. Electronic health record analysts were mock patients who went through the check-in process, were roomed by the nursing staff and technicians, received fake eye exams, and went through checkout. The clinic staff and physicians practiced all of their workflows in as close to a real environment as possible. The physicians and technicians discussed where each would stand, where supplies would be placed in the exam room, and who would document which part of the visit. This strategy was extremely effective. It took the clinic less than two weeks to return to normal volumes and less than a month for physicians to be leaving to go home at the same time as they had prior to the implementation. The clinic continues to work with the electronic health record team to improve its workflow and patient care. The initial hands-on collaboration led to a collaborative culture that has maintained physician and information technology satisfaction.

As this example highlights, physicians can and will change behavior, but hands-on experiences make the transition easier and better. Elbow-to-elbow support or physician hand holding is often discussed with a bit of disdain. However, the need for these directly stems from how physicians learn. They must do it themselves, and they want someone there making sure they do it right. For most physicians, once they learn a skill, they no longer need or want that level of support. A temporary investment in supporting physicians while they learn a new behavior goes far to facilitate behavior change and long-term engagement. Developing a plan in a boardroom and then sending physicians off to implement it is unlikely to work and is even less likely to lead to long-term engagement. Collaborators need to take the lead in ensuring physicians get hands-on experiences; most physicians don't realize that is how they have been trained to learn.

Once a group has learned to Continuously ACT, they need to longitudinally trend/track their shared indicators of success. The metrics should be trended against historic performance with established goals. The best ways to share this information are covered in depth in Chapter 6. The group should regularly, at least quarterly, evaluate the information about shared indicators of success to create actionable knowledge through collaborative communication. Trending of metrics to just look at a graph will not create long-term improvements.

Frequently, gains will plateau, or initial interventions won't reach desired goals. This creates a challenge when engaging physicians. Since they are a group of doers, they quickly tire of reviewing data without making progress toward goals. Additionally, lack of perceived behavioral control is significantly demotivating for physicians. Being shown that they aren't making progress gets translated into "progress can't be made," and they stop the activities that will drive successful outcomes. Unfortunately, this is when administration frequently doubles down on explaining why the project is important. They focus on the impact to the institution, the provider, the patient, and so on. This increases subjective norms, and possibly increases how important the physician believes the outcomes are. But once physicians agree on a shared outcome, the value of the outcome rarely diminishes (especially when it involves improved patient care). So, doubling down on the importance of the outcomes does more harm than good. The increased level of importance may make the goal seem even less achievable. Therefore, the aspect that needs to be managed when outcomes aren't improving is the physicians' belief that it can be controlled and that they can do the work to control it.

Tackling perceived behavioral control can be difficult when things are not going well or not improving. To maintain engagement in these circumstances, you must move the physicians away from "it cannot be done and I don't know how to do it" toward "it is possible and I know exactly what to do." There are three main ways to increase the belief that it can be done. The first is to find success stories from outside your institution. These success stories then need to be shared with the physicians. The stories can be published articles, videos, or a presentation by a knowledge expert. The second is to find success stories inside your institution. Maybe one physician is meeting the goal or one unit/clinic is being successful. Highlight and publish those stories. Give them a venue to present what is working for them. The third is simulation. Have the physicians perform the needed behavior in a simulated environment. Adjust the environment till they can complete the tasks successfully. This will likely identify barriers to completing the tasks in the real environment, but it will add to the physician's belief that it can be done. Increasing the physicians' belief that they know exactly what to do is accomplished by hands-on educational activities. The activities need to be as individualized to the physician as possible and focus on performing their steps. Simulations and scenario-based training are beneficial, but supported real-world experience is most likely to be successful. For example, if you are implementing voice-to-text for clinical documentation, you can do an education session where the surgeon does a pre-operative clinic note and then does a postoperative note in a classroom setting. This will help the physician's confidence, but it isn't a true representation of what it will be like in a busy clinic or noisy surgeon's lounge. To truly tackle perceived behavioral control, a support person should be in the clinic and the surgeon's lounge the first time a provider uses the technology. The support person can troubleshoot problems and remind the surgeon of the little details they forgot from classroom training. After all, it is hard to believe something can't be done after you have already done it.

Meeting agendas need to transition from talking about data to exploring barriers and sharing success. Continuing with the voice-to-text example, rather than reviewing the adoption data, the meeting agenda could be a 15 minute presentation by Dr. Smith, who heavily uses the technology and goes home earlier each day because of it. The group could observe Dr. Smith using the voice-to-text application to see how a successful person uses the application. The group could then debrief about what they learned. The next meeting might be a training session where the group goes through the training and the physicians are able to provide feedback. The agenda could be that the members divide up into small groups to go to different clinics/units to see whether microphones are strategically deployed and talk to physicians about why they are or are not using the technology.

Keep in mind that before group members are deployed into clinical or operational settings, they must first believe that the behavior is possible. Therefore, it is important that the first meetings focus on this topic: individuals/teams can be successful. Successes need to be continuously highlighted as barriers are identified and overcome. The harder the transition, the more engagement depends on creating a belief that the transition can be achieved. Hands-on experiences help physicians learn how to make the transition.

Long-term engagement is sustained through action and requires that administrators/collaborators be mindful of what increases the likelihood that physicians will take actions that support the long-term goals.

Reference

1. Levitt, S. D. and J. A. List. 2011. Was there really a Hawthorne effect at the Hawthorne plant? An analysis of the original illumination experiments. *American Economic Journal: Applied Economics*. Vol. 3, 1, 224–238.

Chapter 10

Communicating Return on Investment in Healthcare

Key Concepts

- There are five areas of return on investment (ROI) in health care:
  - Patient outcomes
  - Clinical delivery
  - Operational effectiveness
  - Health system reputation
  - Financial success
- Demonstrating ROI in more than one of the five areas of return is the most effective way to influence all stakeholders, as they may be motivated by different factors.
- Predicting the ROI is an effective way to select which path to take. ROI can be predicted and used in advance of beginning an initiative.

"No margin. No mission." I don't remember where or when I first heard the phrase, but I distinctly remember the feeling. I was angry. Why are we talking about money when we are supposed to be focused on patient care? The reaction was naïve, and as my understanding about the complexity of the U.S. healthcare system grew, I began to understand why they were talking about margin. I have come to understand that health systems, hospitals, and clinics do run the risk of closing, and that their closing does negatively impact whole communities, both economically and with regard to health. No matter how crass or heartless it seems, healthcare administrators and clinicians need to worry about margin. However, I still have not come to embrace the phrase "No margin. No mission." I believe it is a defensive phrase, something you would use when you are not in control and losing a fight. Granted, there is a lot we do not control in our healthcare system, but I do not think we lack all control. We must be good, active stewards of our revenue, and we must protect our hospitals and clinics from closing. But we must do it in a way that improves care, not just keeps the doors open. Thus, I would prefer to use the phrase, "Protect your margin. Enhance your mission." The work to improve sepsis outcomes explored in early Chapters 4 and 5 is a great example of this focus.

I led the sepsis improvement task force for about 18 months. In that time, we transitioned from a group with data to a high-functioning team that was achieving shared outcomes. After approximately 18 months, I transitioned institutions, and the task force continued to make improvements. The group was able to show remarkable ROI. A task force publication, of which I was a co-author, studied 1401 patients with sepsis before the task force's interventions and 1331 with sepsis after the intervention.[1] The intervention was described as one "that focused on earlier identification of sepsis, early antimicrobial administration, and an educational program that was disseminated throughout all hospital units and services." The program resulted in a 30% decrease in the odds of a patient dying, 1.07 fewer days in the intensive care unit per patient, and a reduction in average length of stay by 2.15 days. Additionally, there was a $1,949 cost saving per admission.

The data used in the paper was tracked from the beginning of the project[1]. The primary metric was the time to antibiotic administration. However, the team also closely followed the length of stay, use of the intensive care unit, and mortality rate. Cost was a secondary concern, but was reviewed as a lagging indicator. Cost being a secondary concern is one of the best things about health care. Interventions can focus on improving care and the health of populations without regard for the relative financial impact. However, to remain viable long term, changes must be fundable and bring value. The sepsis task force continued to make improvements mostly because they were saving lives, but the $2.7 million in cost savings didn't hurt the cause. When calculating and demonstrating ROI, it is important to do it in ways that matter to all the groups involved. It should be done in a way that demonstrates value for both clinicians and administrators.

Thus far in this book, we have covered how to successfully engage physicians, how to get them on board, and how to help them adopt new actions to support shared outcomes. After all that hard work, you need to show that your efforts had an impact and created value. You have to show that you protected your margin and enhanced your mission. You need to show value. To show value, you have to make it obvious that the impact was worth the investment. The comparison of impact to investment is the ROI. Classically, ROI is done in financial terms and is calculated as

$$\text{Return on investment}\,(\%) = \frac{\text{revenue} - \text{investment}}{\text{investment}} \times 100$$

However, financial ROI typically does not resonate with physicians and does not address enhancing your mission. Instead, ROI needs to be presented in a manner that matters to physicians, other clinicians, chief executive officers (CEOs), and chief financial officers (CFOs), and demonstrating such in a way that keeps the project funded; change is rarely free. We have found that there are five areas that can be used to show impact in health care: patient outcomes, clinical delivery, operational effectiveness, health system reputation, and financial success. With modern reimbursement models, there is frequently overlap between the five areas. However, for clarity we will treat them as distinct areas.

Before we get into specifics, there is an essential concept we need to cover. That concept is the number needed to treat (NNT). NNT is one of the most meaningful measurements that result from clinical trials. It is the number of subjects who need to receive the treatment for one subject to have a benefit. It describes not only the effectiveness of the intervention, but also its value. The smaller the NNT, the higher its effectiveness and value. For example, if administering a new medication means that 20 people out of 100 will have a heart attack instead of 30 people out of 100, then 10 people out of 100 benefited from the new medication. You calculate the NNT by dividing the number treated by the number who benefit. In this example, 100 people were treated and 10 benefited, so 100/10. Therefore, the NNT is 10. If the medication had only reduced heart attacks to 26, the number of people benefiting would be 4, and the NNT would be 25. This concept of total cost/effort divided by benefit is, in our opinion, the best way to express ROI for non-financial considerations.

Patient outcomes cover a variety of negative clinical events, gaps in care, and patient satisfaction. Examples include hospital-acquired conditions (infections, pressure ulcers, etc.), missing prescriptions for chronic conditions, missed mammograms and colonoscopies, and the patient's likelihood to recommend the facility/provider. The specific outcomes for an initiative should be identified as a shared indicator of success and defined as a shared metric. From that metric, you can define the patient outcomes ROI in terms of dollars spent to prevent or achieve a specific outcome.

$$\text{Patient outcome ROI}(\$) = \frac{\text{revenue from initiative} - \text{cost of the initiative}}{\text{number of events prevented or achieved}}$$

Improvement in patient outcomes may generate no revenue, so the patient outcome ROI is often negative, which indicates that preventing an event or achieving a positive outcome is an expense. For instance, a project to prevent pressure ulcers by providing special mattresses to high-risk patients costs \$50,000 and generates no revenue. Over the life of the mattresses, the project prevents 100 pressure ulcers, so the calculation would be

$$\text{Patient outcome ROI}(\$) = \frac{0 - \$50,000}{100 \text{ pressure ulcers prevented}}$$

$$= \frac{-\$500}{1 \text{ pressure ulcer prevented}}$$

Some would argue that this calculation should include cost avoidance; we, however, strongly disagree. Cost avoidance is notoriously hard to calculate accurately and can easily be used make a poor financial decision seem reasonable. We recommend calculating a true dollar cost with regard to patient outcomes. True dollar costs can be calculated accurately and demonstrate the financial impact of supporting the improvement. Those accurate costs can then be compared with an estimated cost avoidance to make decisions that protect a systems margin but may appear to be costly at first glance. In the above example, losing $500 to prevent a pressure ulcer may seem like a bad financial decision. However, the incremental cost of treating a pressure ulcer is estimated to be between $2,000 and $20,000 depending on severity.[2] With those high costs as a reference, a loss of $500 is a much better financial decision than a loss of more than $2,000.

Clinical delivery involves all aspects of care delivery, including clinical efficiency and clinician satisfaction. Examples include nurse staffing, patient volumes, door-to-balloon time in severe heart attacks, time from discharge order to patient discharge, barcode medication administration, length of stay, and nurse/physician turnover.

$$\text{Clinical delivery ROI}(\$) = \frac{\text{revenue from initiative} - \text{cost of the initiative}}{\text{improvement}}$$

Most clinical delivery measures improve by getting smaller, but not all. This is important when calculating the ROI. You want improvement to be a positive number; therefore, improvement needs to be calculated differently if having more of something is success versus when having less of something is success. When improvement means having less, improvement should be calculated as

$$\text{Improvement} = \text{baseline performance} - \text{current performance}$$

For example, when considering length of stay and mortality, improvement is based on these numbers decreasing, so you would use this formula. When improvement means having more, such as increasing compliance with screenings such as mammograms and colonoscopies or use of safe practices such as barcode medication administration, improvement should be calculated as

$$\text{Improvement} = \text{current performance} - \text{baseline performance}$$

Another important consideration with clinical delivery ROI is that it is most meaningful and clear when performance is measured in percentages instead of rates, and counts instead of averages. To illustrate this, we will use barcode medication administration and excess length of stay as examples. Barcode medication administration is the use of barcode scanners in hospitals to scan medications and patients to ensure that patients receive the correct medication. High compliance with its use has been demonstrated to reduce errors when administering medications. Compliance can be expressed as a rate or a percentage. For example, if nurses are compliant 60 out of 100 times, the compliance rate is 0.6, and the percentage compliant is 60%. This may seem to be a minor difference, but its effect on the clarity of the ROI calculation is significant. Let's compare the two when an improvement effort increased the compliance from 60 out of 100 to 80 out of 100. First, we will use the "when improvement means having more" equation:

$$\text{Improvement} = \text{current performance} - \text{baseline performance}$$

Thus

$$\text{Improvement} = 0.8 - 0.6 = 0.2$$

or

$$\text{Improvement} = 80\% - 60\% = 20\%$$

Now, let's say the initiative resulted in no revenue and cost $20,000 in education resource and $40,000 of nursing time for a total cost of $60,000. The calculations for clinical delivery ROI are

$$\text{Clinical delivery ROI}(\$) = \frac{\$0 - \$60,000}{0.2}$$

$$= -\$300,000$$

and

$$\text{Clinical delivery ROI}(\$) = \frac{\$0 - \$60,000}{20\%}$$

$$= -\$3,000 \text{ per } 1\% \text{ improvement}$$

Obviously, a $3,000 expense per 1% improvement provides more informa-tion than a calculation of –$300,000, because you are able to see both the cost and the benefit. The same holds true for counts versus averages. Length of stay can be expressed as the average number of hospital days per patient or the total number of patient days for the facility. It is most frequently expressed as an average; for example, the average length of stay (ALOS) is 5.2 days/patient. Excess length of stay is the actual length of stay as com-pared with a benchmark/goal. Using 5.2 days/patient as the actual ALOS and a benchmark of 4.8 days/patient, the excess patient days are 0.4/patient. However, that 0.4 days/patient would be very different if the system had 1,000 patients versus 10,000 patients. Let's compare an improvement proj-ect that cost $300,000 and reduced the actual ALOS to benchmark for both those health systems. Both have the same 0.4 days/patient reduction in ALOS, so the ROI calculation based on ALOS would be

$$\text{Clinical delivery ROI}(\$) = \frac{\$0 - \$300,000}{0.4 \text{ patient days per patient}}$$

$$= -\$750,000 \text{ for 1 patient day per patient}$$

For the health system with 1,000 patients, 0.4 days/patient multiplied by 1,000 patients is 400 days. So, the ROI based on reduced days is

$$\text{Clinical delivery ROI}(\$) = \frac{\$0 - \$300,000}{400 \text{ reduced patient days}}$$

$$= -\$750 \text{ per reduced patient day}$$

For the health system with 10,000 patients, they will have reduced patient days by 4,000, and their ROI calculation is

$$\text{Clinical delivery ROI}(\$) = \frac{\$0 - \$300,000}{4000 \text{ reduced patient days}}$$

$$= -\$75 \text{ per reduced patient day}$$

The first calculation is not mathematically incorrect—both health systems could project that the additional investment of $450,000 would give them an additional 0.6 reduction in ALOS. But this is more of a predictive calculation based on a number of assumptions that may or may not be true. It is not a true ROI calculation, because it does not provide meaningful knowledge about the true cost and benefits of the intervention. Using the second calculation provides more clarity, and clarity in clinical delivery ROI is paramount. Clinicians, especially physicians, need to understand the ROI calculations as easily as the CFO does to foster engagement.

Operational effectiveness encompasses operational efficiency and employee satisfaction. Examples include bed turnover time in the operating room, average time to clean a room, employee turnover, operating room use, no-show rates, and number of same-day appointments. The ROI calculations for operational effectiveness parallel those for clinical care delivery. The ROI calculation is

$$\text{Operational effectiveness ROI}(\$) = \frac{\text{revenue from initiative} - \text{cost of the initiative}}{\text{improvement}}$$

The same need to keep improvement positive, as well as the need to use percentages and counts, applies. A simple example would be a clinic's new appointment reminder system that sends texts to patients' phones to remind them about their appointments a few days ahead of time. In this example, the reminder system costs $50,000/year and reduces no-show rates from 15% to 10%. The office schedules 100,000 appointments per year. The improvement can be calculated as a percentage reduction or as a visit count. When possible, we encourage using the count, since it gives the clearest description of ROI. Since improvement would mean fewer no-shows, we will use the improvement calculation for when less is success.

$$\text{Improvement} = \text{baseline performance} - \text{current performance}$$

Therefore,

$$\text{Improvement} = (100,000 \text{ visits} \times 15\% \text{ no-shows}) - (100,000 \text{ visits} \times 10\% \text{ no-shows})$$

$$= 5,000 \text{ no-show visits prevented}$$

On average, a visit to the clinic generates $60 in revenue, so the 5,000 extra visits where patients attended generated an additional $300,000 in revenue. In addition to the $50,000 per year software cost, an average visit to the clinic cost the clinic $40. So the total cost is $40×5,000 extra visits plus the software fees for a total cost of $250,000. The operational effectiveness calculation is

$$\text{Operational effectiveness ROI}(\$) = \frac{\$300,000 - \$250,000}{5,000 \text{ no-show visits prevented}}$$

$$= \$10 \text{ per no-show visit prevented}$$

A return of $10 per no-show visit prevented clearly defines a positive financial return for an initiative that should have a positive impact on patient care. If we had used percentage improvement, we would not have been able to use the data that the clinic knew about its revenue and cost per visit. Many operational effectiveness measures could be clinical delivery measures, depending on the viewpoint of an individual group, but since the ROI calculations are parallel, the group's selection won't impact how they should determine the ROI.

Health system reputation is reflective of publicly reported rankings and measures. The amount of publicly reported data is ever increasing. A few well-known sources, such as *U.S. News and World Report*, Healthgrades, and Leapfrog, were once the main places to monitor for your reputation. Now, the Center for Medicare and Medicaid Services (CMS) is publishing data, and multiple groups are republishing it. Consumerism is beginning to take hold, and websites such as Yelp are allowing patients to write reviews and grade health systems/providers. Reputation will not be solely defined by a few key sources in the near future; it will also be defined by how patients share their experiences online.

Given the multiple sources and multiple scoring systems, it can be challenging to distill reputation down to a simple expression of improvement that can be used in an ROI calculation. To address this challenge, you need to choose a simplification approach. The primary approach we recommend is change in a group's specific scoring system; changes in percentile rank should only be used as a secondary measure. We do not recommend judging improvement in reputation by improvement in a subcategory of a scoring system. The vast majority of people will only look at the overall grade. Improvement in ranking is probably a truer measure of an ROI, but again, most of the public will only get to the overall scoring.

For instance, many publicly reported measures from CMS break hospitals into three categories: worse than the national rate, no different from the national rate, and better than the national rate. Worse than the national rate is the bottom 2%–5% of performers, and better than the national rate is the top 2%–5% of performers. Moving from the bottom 10% of hospitals to the top 10% likely reflects huge quality gains, yet the hospital's final score remains "no different from the national rate," and thus has no impact on the hospital's reputation for most of the public. CMS's categories are the extreme, and most other scoring systems would improve when a health system moved from the bottom 10% to the top 10%. However, it illustrates the point that significant gains in clinical delivery and operational effectiveness may not significantly impact a health system's reputation, and this needs to be considered as a unique entity for ROI.

Given that reputation is frequently presented publicly in broad categories, we need to use the reciprocal equation to clinical delivery and operational effectiveness, because improvement will frequently be zero, and that shouldn't be in the denominator. Therefore, the reputation ROI is calculated by:

$$\text{Reputation ROI}(\text{gains per \$}) = \frac{\text{improvement}}{\text{revenue from initiative} - \text{cost of the initiative}}$$

Using the reciprocal equation is necessary, given the chance that your initiative will not affect a metric with a wide definition of "average." However, it provides less clarity when used for decision-making.

Taking a look at an online rating site sheds light on reporting ROI for reputation. For this example, we will use Yelp. At the time of this publication, Yelp is combining patient ratings with publicly available ratings from Medicare. The site allows users to write reviews and grade their experience using a five-star system. It also publishes public data from Medicare on emergency department wait times, physician communication, and how quiet rooms are at the hospital. The patient ratings are on a 1–5-point scale, wait times are in minutes, and communication and quiet rooms are rated as below average, average, and above average. The following example will help explain how to tackle these different measures.

A hospital wants to improve its physician communication scores from average to above average, so it starts a new initiative at discharge by adding a bright orange sheet to the patient's discharge papers with their physician's contact numbers on it and instructions about when to call. The hospital follows publicly reported data and reviews on Yelp. Their star rating goes from 2.5 to 4, with multiple people commenting that they knew just whom to call after discharge. Several people also commented that knowing whom to call prevented them from returning to the emergency department. The average wait time in the emergency department was also down to 26 minutes from 30 minutes. A review of patient volumes in the emergency department showed that return visits to the emergency department within 72 hours of discharge were down by 100 visits. The physician communication score remains an average. The hospital's CFO determines that the revenue lost from the fall in emergency department visits is $50,000 and the cost of the discharge initiative was $10,000. The reputation ROI calculations are

$$\text{Reputation ROI(gains per \$)} = \frac{4 \text{ stars on Yelp} - 2.5 \text{ stars on Yelp}}{-\$50,000 - \$10,000}$$

$$= 1 \text{ star on Yelp per } \$40,000 \text{ spent}$$

and

$$\text{Reputation ROI(gains per \$)} = \frac{30 \text{ minute wait} - 26 \text{ minute wait}}{-\$50,000 - \$10,000}$$

$$= 1 \text{ minute less average wait per } \$15,000 \text{ spent}$$

and

$$\text{Reputation ROI(gains per \$)} = \frac{\text{no change in physician communication}}{-\$50,000 - \$10,000}$$

$$= \text{no change in physician communication}$$
$$\text{for } \$60,000 \text{ spent}$$

The initiative had no impact on the target aspect of the hospital's reputation, physician communication. However, it improved its ratings on a popular consumer rating site and is reported to have a more efficient emergency department. The initiative did have a return with regard to the hospital's reputation. Calculating the return for various public measures is often needed to truly determine the impact of an initiative on a system's/provider's reputation.

Financial success is the best-known ROI calculation. It is the creation of margin. Whether a health system is for-profit or not-for-profit, it is critical that revenue exceeds expenses. The excess revenue is margin. Calculating the financial ROI for any initiative is a straightforward calculation using the following equation:

$$\text{Financial success ROI}(\%) = \frac{\text{revenue from initiative} - \text{cost of the initiative}}{\text{cost of the initiative}} \times 100$$

The purpose of this calculation is not to determine how much an initiative will contribute to a system's overall margin, but to describe the magnitude of the initiative's financial impact versus the investment. Determining the revenue and cost from an initiative is not always simple; frequently, it is quite challenging. However, the financial success ROI can heavily influence decision-making. The prevention of no-show visits described above can be used to illustrate this point. The revenue was $300,000 and the cost was $250,000, so the financial success ROI calculation is

$$\text{Financial success ROI}(\%) = \frac{\$300,000 - \$250,000}{\$250,000} \times 100 = 20\%$$

A 20% return makes it obvious that the initiative was good for the bottom line.

Calculating the magnitude of impact versus the absolute impact is important for three reasons. First, healthcare revenue and cost calculations are likely estimates. The reimbursement system in the United States makes it very difficult to get exact figures. Second, when you approach it from a position of protecting your margin, the most significant aspect is that the ROI is positive. If it can't be positive, the magnitude needs to be small. Third, a contribution to margin calculation can be misleading; a million-dollar project that contributes $50,000 to the bottom line doesn't have the same return as a $250,000 project that provides $50,000 to the bottom line.

Independently, the five types of ROI are effective at describing the outcome of an investment. However, using all five (or as many as apply) as a portfolio paints a much better picture of an initiative's impact. Done well, it creates a picture understood by all stakeholders. The results discussed at the beginning of this chapter are perfect to demonstrate this point. The main patient outcome metric was mortality. During the intervention period, more than 93 deaths were prevented. The initiative created no new revenue, and the cost of task force time, clinician education, and formulary change was estimated at $1,500,000. Therefore, the patient outcome ROI is

$$\text{Patient outcome ROI}(\$) = \frac{0 - \$1,500,000}{93 \text{ deaths prevented}}$$

$$= \frac{-\$16,129}{1 \text{ death prevented}}$$

The primary clinical delivery measurement was length of stay. The average length of stay was 15.6 prior to the intervention and 13.1 after. The clinical delivery ROI in terms of length of stay is

$$\text{Clinical delivery ROI}(\$) = \frac{\$0 - \$1,500,000}{1,331 \times (15.6 - 13.1) \text{ reduced patient days}}$$

$$= -\$451 \text{ per reduced patient day}$$

The group's key operational effectiveness measure was days in the critical care unit. The measure could also be considered a secondary clinical delivery metric. Days needed in the critical care unit fell from a baseline of 6.6 days to 5.5 days. The operational effectiveness ROI is

$$\text{Operational effectiveness ROI}(\$) = \frac{\$0 - \$1,500,000}{1,331 \times (6.6 - 5.5) \text{ reduced critical care days}}$$

$$= -\$1,025 \text{ per reduced critical care day}$$

Sepsis mortality was not a publicly reportable measure at the time, and thus, there is no reputation ROI to calculate. The financial success ROI is straightforward:

$$\text{Financial success ROI}(\%) = \frac{\$0 - \$1,500,000}{\$1,500,000} \times 100 = -100\%$$

The effort was 100% cost, which was expected, since the focus was on reducing deaths. At 100% cost, the intervention added $1,127 to each of the 1,331 sepsis admissions. Analyzing the four ROIs demonstrates what that money purchased.

Sepsis Improvement Task Force—$1,500,000 Investment	
Population Impacted: 1,331 Septic Patients	
Return on investment category	Return on investment
Patient outcome	−$16,129 per death prevented
Clinical delivery	−$451 per reduced patient day
Operational effectiveness	−$1,025 per reduced critical care day
Financial success	−100%

The portfolio of ROI shows an expensive intervention that had significant impact across multiple domains and generated no revenue. It was clearly effective in non-financial realms, but a 100% financial loss is concerning. However, cost avoidance for those 1,331 admissions was estimated at $2,600,000. With the addition of the cost avoidance, the portfolio of ROI clearly shows that the Sepsis Task Force and its activities protected the institution's margin while enhancing its mission.

As demonstrated above, retrospective ROI analyses can demonstrate the impact of an initiative or intervention. But, ROI calculations don't need to be retrospective. They can be predictive. Predictive ROI calculations, when done well, are an effective device to help engage physicians in decision-making. The key to high-quality ROI predictions is an earnest attempt to project likely gains or losses. As with all projections, there will be inaccuracies in the ROI predictions. High-quality predictions will generate high-quality knowledge to help you make the right decision, but are unlikely to be highly accurate.

High-quality ROI predictions have four key characteristics. They are based on systematic research or pilot data, conservative, and localized, and have clearly defined assumptions. Without these characteristics, they are informed guesses at best.

Systematic research likely occurred at another institution. The study may be published in a peer-reviewed journal or presented at a conference, but it has a clear intervention group and a defined control group. The control group may be historic or concurrent, but it provides a baseline. The defined baseline makes determining the effect of the intervention straightforward. The difference between the intervention group and the control group is "improvement" from the intervention. Remember to use the right improvement equation from earlier in the chapter. Pilot data is based on interventions at your institution and generally uses historic controls. Improvement is calculated as previously described.

The distinction between pilot data and research data is important with regard to localization. Local data, (data from your institution), does not need to be adjusted. However, data from another institution should be adjusted for your population. For example, if the research study had a baseline readmission rate of 15% with an improvement to 10%, and your institution has a baseline of 20%, you have to adjust your improvement calculation. You have the choice of using the absolute improvement of 5% (15%–10%) or the relative improvement of 33% ((15%–10%)/15%). You cannot make the assumption that the intervention will reduce your readmission rate to 10%.

In this example, you could localize your projections to an absolute improvement of 5% (20%– 15%) or 6.67% (20%×33%) improvement depending on the adjustment you choose. This choice should be the conservative choice. Sometimes the absolute calculation will be less; at other times it will be the relative calculation. Use the smaller value for gains and the larger value for losses. Using the conservative calculation makes it easier to defend your calculations and makes it more likely that you will achieve your projections.

We also recommend using a localization factor in your calculations. By this, we mean making the assumption that you will not be as successful as the research or pilot group. Rarely do local projects work as well as the published data or small pilots. A factor of 0.75 is a good starting point for gains and 1.25 for losses, but it is better to use your actual experience. Track how well you do compared with the goals from the literature and pilots. Over time, you will be able to more accurately calculate your localization factor.

This localization factor is your first assumption. You need to put your assumptions front and center. Your assumptions should be written out and included any time you present your ROI predictions. For example, you should include, "For these calculations we assumed that we would be 75% as effective as the literature, with 25% additional costs." Additional assumptions may include: patient populations are similar; there will be no additional physician/nursing/technology cost; we can use out current technology infrastructure; and so on. It is impossible to list all the possible assumptions, but you should clearly define any ideas or facts you used to generate your calculations.

Based on these characteristics, the equations for project ROI are

Patient outcome ROI ($)

$$= \frac{(\text{revenue from initiative} \times \text{gain factor}) - (\text{cost of the initiative} \times \text{loss factor})}{\text{conservative number of events prevented or achieved} \times \text{gain factor}}$$

Clinical delivery ROI $(\$)$

$$= \frac{(\text{revenue from initiative} \times \text{gain factor}) - (\text{cost of the initiative} \times \text{loss factor})}{\text{conservative improvement} \times \text{gain factor}}$$

Operational effectiveness ROI $(\$)$

$$= \frac{(\text{revenue from initiative} \times \text{gain factor}) - (\text{cost of the initiative} \times \text{loss factor})}{\text{conservative improvement} \times \text{gain factor}}$$

Reputation ROI $(\text{gains per } \$)$

$$= \frac{\text{improvement} \times \text{gain factor}}{(\text{revenue from initiative} \times \text{gain factor}) - (\text{cost of the initiative} \times \text{loss factor})}$$

Financial success ROI $(\%)$

$$= \frac{(\text{revenue from initiative} \times \text{gain factor}) - (\text{cost of the initiative} \times \text{loss factor})}{(\text{cost of the initiative} \times \text{loss factor})} \times 100$$

Adjusting gains down and costs up creates knowledge about an intervention that can facilitate decision-making. If you are more confident about your costs or gains, you can shift the gain and loss factors closer to 1. However, using factors closer to 1 can make decision-making harder. If ROI is projected to be positive for an initiative for which the expected gains are adjusted down 25% and the predicted cost is adjusted up 25%, choosing to execute the initiative is an easier decision, since you will achieve a positive return even with poorly projected outcomes.

Predicting ROI is most valuable when you need to choose between possible interventions, especially when you need to engage physicians in selecting an intervention. Comparing the predicted ROI portfolio provides actionable knowledge that can be used to achieve shared outcomes. For example, you have a shared outcome of reduced readmissions and need to work with your physicians to select the best intervention. The hospital is currently being penalized $750,000 due to having a readmission rate that is worse than the national rate. The team believes that they need to reduce their readmission rate by 3% to avoid next year's penalty. The group has narrowed the intervention options to three. The first is to implement remote patient monitoring, the second is to establish a 7-day follow-up clinic, and the third is to provide patients with free medications at discharge. Based on systematic research, they have an absolute and relative reduction of 5% and 33%, 3% and 25%, and 2% and 20%, respectively, with an estimated cost per discharge of $100, $100, and $50. Your hospital has a baseline readmission rate of 14% with 10,000 admissions per year, and you expect to lose $2,500 in revenue for every readmission prevented. Using a gain factor of 0.75 and a loss factor of 1.25 in your ROI calculations results in the following table.

	Home Monitoring	*7-Day Follow-up Clinic*	*Free Discharge Medications*
Absolute reduction	5%	3%	2%
Relative reduction	33%	25%	20%
Localized reduction	4.66%	3%	2%
Cost per year	$1,000,000	$1,000,000	$500,000
Revenue	−$415,000	−$750,000	−$500,000
Patient outcome ROI ($)	−$4,467 per prevented readmission	−$8,055 per prevented readmission	−$6,667 per prevented readmission
Clinical delivery ROI ($)	−$447,000 per 1% reduction in readmissions	−$806,000 per 1% reduction in readmissions	−$667,000 per 1% reduction in readmissions
Operational effectiveness ROI ($)	N/A	N/A	N/A
Reputation ROI (gain per $)	Improved to "no different from the national rate" for −$1,561,000	No improvement for −$1,813,000	No improvement for −$1,000,000
Financial success ROI (%)	−125%	−145%	−160%

Assumptions: For these calculations, we assumed that we would be 75% as effective as the literature, with 25% additional costs. We also assumed avoiding the readmission penalty to be equivalent to $750,000 in revenue. After localization and adjustment for the gain factor, only home monitoring achieved the reduction projected to avoid the readmission penalty.

The ROI portfolio for the three interventions make it clear that although free discharge medications are the cheapest per discharge option, this offers the lowest financial success ROI and the second lowest clinical returns. Additionally, the 7-day follow-up clinic generates the worst clinical returns, despite having a localized reduction that superficially appears to achieve the group's goals. Home monitoring has the best ROI for patient outcomes, clinical delivery, reputation, and financial success. This finding is counterintuitive, since home monitoring has the greatest expected expense at $1,000,000 and over $1,000,000 in lost revenue from lower readmission rates. However, after localization and adjustment for the interventions being 75% as effective as published, only home monitoring achieves the necessary 3% reduction to avoid the $750,000 penalty.

Engaging physicians with tables like the one shown above is straightforward. You walk them through your assumptions and then the calculations for each intervention. The calculations generate sufficient knowledge about the expected impact at your organization to choose the most appropriate action(s). Frequently, the most impactful choice will be clear. When it is not, the pros and cons of each intervention are objectively described. Using this type of predicted ROI portfolio can transform your interactions with physicians. The discussions will be more focused and based on objective measures instead of anecdotes. Be prepared to defend your assumptions and calculations, and when possible, have a physician partner with you while doing the analysis. This will both improve the quality of your analysis and make it easier to defend your results.

Reference

1. Armen S.B., Freer C.V., Showalter J.W., Crook T., Whitener C.J., West C., Terndrup T.E., Grifasi M., DeFlitch C.J., Hollenbeak C.S. Improving outcomes in patients with sepsis. *Am J Med Qual.* 2016 Jan-Feb;31(1):56–63. doi: 10.1177/1062860614551042. Epub 2014 Sep 12.
2. Leaf Healthcare. 2014. *The Financial Impact of Pressure Ulcers*. Pleasanton, CA: Leaf Healthcare.

Summary

To paraphrase one of the first people to read a full draft of this book, "Wow, that was a lot."

We have talked about physician psychology, communication styles, data-driven maturity models, physician executives, and demonstrating return on investment. It *is* a lot and choosing where to start can be daunting. Many of you will be in the middle of projects where it will be difficult to restructure them to follow our guidance. Others will be starting projects and need to focus on getting buy-in instead of focusing on adapting their projects to incorporate the ideas we present. Others will be in countless other situations.

The great thing about this book is that no matter your situation you can begin to apply the lessons we have learned and improve your results. Simply reminding yourself that physicians aren't intentionally being difficult can positively affect your performance in a meeting. Being mindful of their learning style (hands-on and independent), will improve your communication, educational efforts, and behavioral change initiatives. As the quality of your interactions with physicians improve, so will your effectiveness, even if you can't fully apply the maturity model outlined in this book. Data-driven behavioral change is as much about the relationships as the data.

We support the use of technology and advanced computing—we have even been called evangelists for the use of predictive analytics—but the most amazing knowledge is meaningless if you can't engage with your physicians. Our framework for fostering and developing these relationships provides structure to an activity that is truly an art. As with all arts, mastery comes from applying a set of skills until you are able to direct the outcome. Even the most accomplished artist doesn't have perfect technique with every brush stroke. However, they know the image they plan to create and turn a blank canvas into a masterpiece. We have presented a number of skills to master physician engagement. You will need to practice those skills and learn from your experiences to achieve shared outcomes. Once you have mastered how to effectively engage physicians, you will be able to create a new future for your patients. A future based on creating value and improving outcomes.

Our challenge to you is to create a clear vision of the future and then go make it a reality. A healthier community is possible when we engage each other in meaningful ways and together, achieve shared outcomes.

Index

Printed in the United States
by Baker & Taylor Publisher Services